DATA rEVOLUTION

CSC Leading Edge Forum

Paul Gustafson

Sidney Shek

CSC
Falls Church, Virginia, USA

CSC

3170 Fairview Park Drive
Falls Church, Virginia, 22042
United States

Published by Computer Sciences Corporation (www.csc.com),
printed and distributed by Lulu (www.lulu.com).

ISBN 978-0-578-09424-3

DATA rEVOLUTION

ABOUT THE LEADING EDGE FORUM

As part of CSC's Office of Innovation, the Leading Edge Forum (LEF) is a global community whose programs help participants realize business benefits from the use of advanced IT more rapidly.

The LEF works to spot key emerging business and technology trends before others, and identify specific practices for exploiting these trends for business advantage. The LEF draws from a global network of thought leaders and leading practitioners, proven field practices, and a powerful body of research.

LEF Technology Programs give CTOs and senior technologists the opportunity to explore the most pressing technology issues, examine state-of-the-art practices, and leverage CSC's technology experts, alliance programs and events. The reports and papers produced under the LEF are intended to provoke conversations in the marketplace about the potential for innovation when applying technology to advance organizational performance. Visit www.csc.com/lef.

The LEF Executive Programme is a premium, fee-based program that helps CIOs and senior business executives develop into next-generation leaders by using technology for competitive advantage in wholly new ways. Members direct the research agenda, interact with a network of world-class experts, and access topical conferences, study tours, information exchanges and advisory services. Visit lef.csc.com.

WILLIAM KOFF (LEFT)
Vice President and Chief Technology Officer, Office of Innovation

A leader in CSC's technology community, Bill Koff provides vision and direction to CSC and its clients on critical information technology trends, technology innovation and strategic investments in leading edge technology. Bill plays a key role in guiding CSC research, innovation, technology leadership and alliance partner activities, and in certifying CSC's Centers of Excellence and Innovation Centers.
wkoff@csc.com

PAUL GUSTAFSON (RIGHT)
Director, Leading Edge Forum, Technology Programs

Paul Gustafson is an accomplished technologist and proven leader in emerging technologies, applied research and strategy. Paul brings vision and leadership to a portfolio of LEF programs and directs the technology research agenda. Astute at recognizing how technology trends inter-relate and impact business, Paul applies his insights to client strategy, CSC research, leadership development and innovation strategy.
pgustafs@csc.com

In this ongoing series of reports about technology directions, the LEF looks at the role of innovation in the marketplace both now and in the years to come. By studying technology's current realities and anticipating its future shape, these reports provide organizations with the necessary balance between tactical decision-making and strategic planning.

DATA rEVOLUTION

You can access this report via the LEF RSS feed www.csc.com/lefpodcast
or the LEF Web site www.csc.com/lefreports

BYTES TO INSIGHTS

From companies to consumers, people have an insatiable appetite for data and all it can do. We are not only depending on data for movie recommendations and gift ideas but are pushing hard on data for multidisciplinary climate research and energy exploration, roads and buildings that adapt to their environment, more predictive healthcare, new ways to detect fraud, and keeping abreast of consumer sentiment and behavior. There are all sorts of new data and new uses. The data feast is on, and not likely to stop any time soon.

Whereas in the past data was primarily generated in enterprise systems, today's data comes from many additional sources: social networks, blogs, chat rooms, product review sites, communities, Web pages, email, documents, images, videos, music and sensors. It is often chaotic – unstructured – and doesn't fit neatly into the orderly – structured – world of the past. The challenge of the Data rEvolution is to unite and process the data, connect the dots, and glean new insights. And, do all this rapidly.

The Data rEvolution is both a revolution and an evolution. The revolution lies in:

- new kinds of data, both people-generated and machine-generated (e.g., consumer data, query data, sensor data, actuator data)
- massive amounts of data
- complexity of data
- diversity of data
- new ways to organize and manage the data for rapid processing
- new tools for gleaning insights from the data
- new linkages
- data opening up for more widespread analysis, use and experimentation

The evolution lies in the steady advances of the technology base itself – compute and storage platforms, applications, architectures, and the communication networks that tie everything together.

THE ECONOMICS OF DATA

In 2010 *The Economist* asserted that data has become a factor of production, almost on par with labor and capital.[1] Market moves bear this out. How companies and investors are placing their bets on big data and analytics, shown in Figure 1, is a bellwether of the data phenomenon.[2]

There are many different measures of this phenomenon. IDC predicts that the digital universe will be 44 times bigger in 2020 than it was in 2009, totaling a staggering 35 zettabytes.[3] EMC reports that the number of customers storing a petabyte or more of data will grow from 1,000 (reached in 2010) to 100,000 before the end of the decade.[4] By 2012 it expects that some customers will be storing exabytes (1,000 petabytes) of information.[5] In 2010 Gartner reported that enterprise data growth will be 650 percent over the next five years, and that 80 percent of that will be unstructured.[6]

The trick is analyzing the data for new insights to improve business performance. Recognizing this data imperative, enterprises are hiring data scientists even as they cut jobs elsewhere. Data scientists and statisticians are the new cool.

DATA FOR ACTION

Data is ultimately about insights. How are people connecting the data dots to gain new insights? How are they completing the context? Or obtaining a more complete

FOLLOW THE MONEY: ANALYTICS

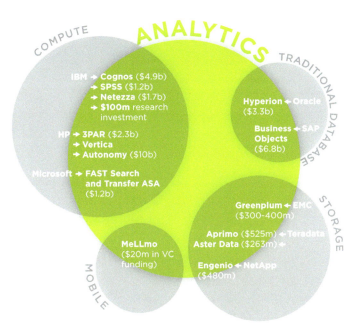

Figure 1 Market acquisitions and funding point to data analytics.
Source: CSC

context? A consumer products company might combine structured financials with unstructured data about what customers are saying online about its products. Discovery – combining and mining the data – is key.

This discovery is marked by new freedom to explore. It's no longer about "what questions do you want your data to answer" and building a data model for that, but "here's the data and what do you want to ask?" Let the data lead.

We are creating a new "sense of things" from all the information we are collecting, processing and reordering, which is helping us model our world. With this, we are creating new approaches to problem solving and more advanced visualization techniques that can help us identify trends, spot crooks, and even guess what we all are thinking. We are developing new ways to enhance multidisciplinary cooperation and collaboration, and simulations to enhance and accelerate R&D, using data to peer inside nanotechnologies, the brain, weather patterns and design changes, and even to ask questions about the nature of the universe. It's all about turning vast quantities of impenetrable, structured and unstructured data into instant, actionable data.

NEW DATA MEANS NEW TOOLS

Given the volume, variety and velocity of data, the tools for analysis are changing. More people can peer into the data in more ways for more meaning. Analytics is no longer confined to a few people working with a subset of data on a small analytics server off in a corner. Today analytics is moving to center stage as more people can access the tools and analyze *all* the data, leveraging data from multiple sources and unleashing the power of a distributed grid of computing resources to do the heavy lifting involved with the analysis. Today's analytics are also moving to the "predictive edge," where the analysis is more time-sensitive, closing in on real-time results. Under the covers, many of today's analytics are using "in-database" techniques that are faster and far more efficient because the data is not moved to a separate analytics server; instead, the analytics are brought to where the data resides.

Consider insurance fraud analysis that was traditionally run, say, every two months. At that point the damage was done – the fraudulent insurance claim had already been paid. This approach was slow and passive. Now insurance companies can run in-database fraud analysis *twice a day*, catching fraudulent claims within hours. Whereas traditional systems were fine-tuned for transactions and batch processing, today we need to sense and respond to changing conditions immediately.

To do this, we need to focus on the data, not the structure. In the past we focused on structured relational databases, predefined relationships, and structured transactional data. Although those don't go away, now we also have reams of unstructured data, untold relationships between the data, and new data coming in all the time – more dynamic data, with multiple contexts, from many sources, both people and machines. We must adopt more flexible, less structured, non-relational approaches.

CHAOTIC, RICH REALITY

This shift in how we handle data reflects the fact that our world is complex and connected in ways we cannot imagine. The Internet has brought all of this complexity to us in a torrent of data that is at once massive, diverse, disorganized and rich in valuable information. It happened in the blink of an eye, it's here to stay, and we have to deal with it.

Further, what happened on the Internet is happening in corporations and governments. There are few rules and virtually no constraints. Every author of content can invent his or her own structure, create his or her own context, and tell his or her own story. Some of the data can be defined as well-structured and some is semi-structured, but much of it is quite unstructured.

Amidst all this diverse data, connections are king. The simple concept of the link is so profound and yet so natural. Linking allows us to connect virtually any set of information together to tell a story; further, the same story can be told in many different ways. To top it off, we're seeing that the connections keep changing. In today's data world, there is no place for the rigid and ordered. Our new data world is a place where chaos runs rampant. This world is free, it is loose, it is not standard, it is us. The data reflects everything that we are.

> Our new data world is a place where chaos runs rampant. This world is free, it is loose, it is not standard, it is us.

The Data rEvolution represents a profound shift on many levels, summarized in Figure 2. This report explores these shifts by examining five areas:

- *Great Expectations: Do More with More (Data)* – How leading organizations living the Data rEvolution are setting new expectations for getting results from data

- *A Changing Foundation: New Methods to Manage Big Data* – New ways to organize and manage massive, diverse data for complex processing using approaches like MapReduce and Hadoop

Figure 2 DATA rEVOLUTION

FROM	TO
Data as a fact of life	Data as a factor of production
Collecting	Connecting
Analyzing	Predicting
Information	Insights
"One version of the truth"	Multiple sources and perspectives
Structured	Unstructured
Relational	Non-relational
Centralized processing	Distributed parallel processing
Terabytes	Petabytes, exabytes, ...
Analytics as niche	Analytics for everyone
Limited participation	An era of experimentation and innovation

Source: CSC

- *The New Alchemy: Connecting the Dots* – New tools and methods for establishing relationships and meaning, including folksonomies, semantics, link analysis, temporal analysis, location-based services and situational intelligence

- *Enabling the Predictive Enterprise: Strategies to Understand, Anticipate and Plan* – New ways to achieve insights through better questions, social discovery, predictive analytics, advanced models and analytics for everyone

- *Seeing Is Believing: Visualization and Visual Analytics* – New methods of visualization and visual analytics to parse the data and literally see new relationships and insights on the fly

As James Gleick writes in *The Information*, information is "the vital principle" of our world.[7] We are a universe of information. We are an economy built more and more on data. Data is disrupting not only business, but how we work with data itself. "Now, as at any moment of technological disruption, he [Gleick] writes, 'the old ways of organizing knowledge no longer work.'"[8]

The Data rEvolution is about leveraging data in new ways. Data is a means to an end for new insights, innovation and connections with people, places and things. Organizations need to tap their treasure trove of data and put it to work like never before.

GREAT EXPECTATIONS:
DO MORE WITH MORE (DATA)

Today's enterprise needs are setting new expectations around data: do more with more. With so much data coming in, organizations are challenged to harness the data in new ways for new insights. Further, we want the analysis now. We operate in real time and we expect our data to do the same.

Yet as technology evolves, there are still many unanswered questions that cannot be addressed with conventional techniques. Wall Street's "flash crash" on May 6, 2010, is one

> **Today's enterprise needs are setting new expectations around data: do more with more.**

small example, where the growing complexity of trading instruments, high-speed trading environments, and trading variables created such a perfect storm that the core cause is still not clear despite the results of a data-intensive government investigation.[9]

Another example is the genome. Once hoped to unlock the mystery of life and give us new ways to cure or eradicate disease, the genome has instead become an enormous information problem. The genome is a rich DNA information exchange that has been happening since life began, so trying to extrapolate and retrace those information flows, and then analyze their impact on future exchanges, makes the flash crash look like a grade school math assignment.

Today no industry is exempt from the challenges – or the opportunities – of the Data rEvolution. Even the U.S.

government has called for all its agencies to have a "Big Data" strategy because of the challenges they'll be facing.[10] Progress is beginning in many fields as organizations seek to derive meaning from data and "complete the context." Whether for discovering more about the world around us, making financial decisions or understanding customer behavior, data is driving our actions more and more.

SCIENCE: EXPLORING OUR WORLD

Science is a natural for the Data rEvolution, where vast amounts of data are analyzed to address some of the planet's most perplexing questions, such as climate change and how to reduce its impact, and the origin of the universe. The democratization of data and better integration methods, coupled with a surge in data volumes, are shifting the science paradigm to a more collaborative, open endeavor. This shift to "open science" is one of necessity, as data sets are too large and problems are too complex to be analyzed by a single entity.

Take global climate change, where scientists are seeking answers to questions in three areas: how climate is changing (e.g., rising temperatures, rising sea levels), the effects of climate change (e.g, the effect of rising sea levels on coastal areas and the people who live there) and actions to take as a result (e.g., whether or not to construct new buildings and bridges near the coast). The analytical modeling to address these questions becomes increasingly sophisticated as you move from understanding the underlying science of climate change to predicting its effects to making decisions about how to respond. "More and more, the big problems in climate relate to specific decisions. As a city manager or policymaker, what do I do?" explains Sharon Hays, vice president in CSC's Office of Science and Engineering who heads the climate change business initiative. "These questions are increasingly influencing the data gathering."

Climate science is a relatively new science that draws the big picture of Earth systems from a diverse set of scientific disciplines that study the atmosphere, weather patterns, oceans, land masses, biology, chemistry and space. Models of Earth systems require enormous amounts of computational power and detailed longitudinal data. Though organizations have been collecting weather data for years, it is not accurate or widespread enough for climate research. At the same time, the newer, more accurate global data does not exist over a long enough period to create models that can reasonably make long-term predictions about the complex interactions between Earth systems. However, this will improve as more satellites come online, more land- and sea-based sensors report new data, and large cooperative research efforts combine their resources. Data at the U.S. National Climatic Data Center already tops 300 terabytes and is expected to increase at roughly 80 terabytes per year.[11]

One example of a large cooperative effort is the U.S. Ocean Observatories Initiative (OOI), under the National Science Foundation, which will instrument the seafloor off the Pacific Northwest coast. (See Figure 3.) These ocean floor sensors will measure physical, chemical, geological and biological variables in the ocean and seafloor. The OOI has built a data distribution network in collaboration with the U.S. National Oceanic and Atmospheric Administration (NOAA), which will provide data in the formats most typically used.[12] Data will be reported to scientists on land, creating a virtual observatory.

"Instead of going out on a ship and taking measurements, you'll be able to sit in an ivory tower and study these raw data sets," says Conrad Lautenbacher, vice president of science programs at CSC and former director of NOAA. "The intent is to create data sets that

can be used by a variety of disciplines. In the future, imagine connecting climate data to health data to improve our understanding of climate effects on people. I view climate change as a grand challenge that affects the chain of life. It is about both having the right data and interpreting what it means."

NOAA is archiving the nation's environmental and climate data that is essential for understanding climate change. CSC is developing the information management system for this, the Comprehensive Large Array-data Stewardship System (CLASS), a secure data storage and distribution system operated by NOAA. CLASS is a digital library of historical data from NOAA's Polar-orbiting Operational Environmental Satellites. CLASS provides advanced capabilities for finding and obtaining critical environmental

Figure 3 The regional component of the Ocean Observatories Initiative is called Regional Scale Nodes. RSN will extend continuous high bandwidth and power to a network of instruments widely distributed across and above the Pacific seafloor off the Washington and Oregon coasts. This network of nodes will provide a constant stream of data in real time from the ocean and seafloor so scientists can better understand the world's oceans. The network will supply 10 gigabits per second of bandwidth and 8 kilowatts of power to each instrumented node upon commissioning in 2014. The University of Washington is leading the RSN effort.
Source: OOI Regional Scale Nodes and Center for Environmental Visualization, University of Washington

data that is stored in a variety of media dating back to the late 1970s. As the major subcontractor to prime contractor Diversified Global Partners JV LLC, CSC works to process and store the CLASS data and make it available to the public. Systems like CLASS enable organizations to save money on energy and reduce potential adverse impacts of a changing climate. (See Figure 4.)

Along these lines, one response to climate change is more eco-friendly and efficient energy use. Using renewable energy resources like wind and hydropower in lieu of fossil fuels demands a steady stream of real-time data to make

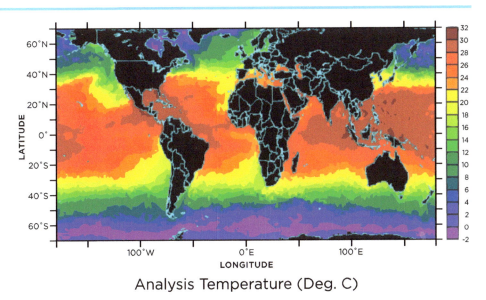

Analysis Temperature (Deg. C)

Figure 4 This map presents global sea surface temperatures for June 23, 2011. It was generated from data in NOAA CLASS and is available at www.class.noaa.gov. Source: NOAA

all the inter-related systems before that wellbore is drilled. The recent discovery of large new gas plays in shale formations in the United States provides the opportunity to use cleaner natural gas, but these wellbores are more difficult to drill and complete. Financial and petrotechnical modeling to determine the most effective and safest way to unleash the natural gas trapped in the rock formations requires a much more sophisticated approach to understanding the data. What is required is a much wider view of all related information about the areas to be produced, which is commonly called the Whole Earth Model.

The Whole Earth Model is a data fusion and visualization technique and integrated data management system that lets a collaborating team of geophysicists, petroleum engineers, facilities engineers, and financial managers examine an oil or gas field by looking at a surface and geologic model with all of the wellbores, pipelines, surface equipment and seismic data shown so that they can make effective decisions using all the information at hand. For example, maybe the petroleum engineers want to drill a well in a certain location, but the facilities people point out that there are no pipelines in that area, and the ocean floor drops off precipitously so the cost of running a pipeline to that well would be very high. The financial people can pull up data to estimate

decisions "every hour, every second" about how to manage the renewable energy grid, as Portugal has learned in its transformation to using more renewable energy.[13] More broadly, a global move towards infrastructure transformation (roads, bridges, water system, public transportation, etc.) that minimizes carbon emissions and is resistant to cyber-attack is under discussion, with particular focus in the United States and Australia. An intelligent infrastructure laden with sensors can adapt so that buildings use less energy, for example, or the infrastructure self-corrects for climate-induced change.[14] This is a sweeping proposition, in which data plays a central role.

A broader perspective is also being taken in the science of energy exploration, where it's no longer as simple as just drilling a hole into the Earth but is now about understanding

the costs of various options to get the production to the surface. The problem is even more interesting when the participants are located in Scotland, Indonesia and the United States and the complex data sets need to be simultaneously viewed at collaboration centers in all of these locations. CSC's energy clients like Petrohawk Energy are deeply involved in these promising new areas, and are using enterprise intelligence tools to understand the relative impacts of different drilling and production strategies.

No doubt the biggest data project on the planet is at CERN, Europe's nuclear research facility. CERN collects unprecedented amounts of data from its Large Hadron Collider (LHC) to study unresolved questions in particle physics. The LHC produces roughly 15 petabytes of data annually – enough to fill more than 1.7 million dual-layer DVDs a year.[15] The resulting data feeds hundreds of experiments conducted by some 10,000 physicists at 200 institutes worldwide. These experiments include exploring the origin of mass, anti-matter, and the forces of nature (e.g., gravity).

To provide the data, CERN collaborates with institutions worldwide to operate a distributed computing and data storage infrastructure called the Worldwide LHC Computing Grid (WLCG). This grid integrates thousands of computers and storage systems in over 140 data centers in 35 countries, enabling "a collaborative computing environment on a scale never seen before."[16] The grid gives physicists near real-time access to the data, and the power to process it.[17]

The LHC systems and data are designed for collaboration because early on it was clear that CERN could not assemble (fund) the necessary computing power, but its partner universities and laboratories had access to national and or regional computing facilities. Thus the CERN grid was born, based on two main global grids (the European Grid Infrastructure in Europe and the Open Science Grid in the United States) and their associated regional and national grids, portending a trend toward greater distributed processing and data sharing when data sets are too large and complex for a single entity to handle. Further, as the data grows, a distributed grid is easier to expand than a monolithic computer.[18]

The LHC streams two particle beams in opposite directions in a 27-kilometer circular tunnel buried beneath the French-Swiss border. When the protons in the beams collide, at almost the speed of light, the collisions – 100 million per second – generate an enormous amount of data. In split second fashion, most of the data must be rejected – only one of one million collisions (data) is kept. CERN's massive grid and distributed processing framework analyze the data and make the select/reject decision.

Rapidly processing and reducing enormous amounts of data using a grid of processors to glean insights is applicable to many industries. Organizations are trying to gain deeper understanding from the big data streams they are facing. They may not be smashing protons to generate the data, but they do need to "instrument their information systems" so they can capture, sample and analyze the data essential to their own grand challenges. CERN is a premier example of this and of how today's big data problems demand a new data infrastructure.

> **Organizations need to "instrument their information systems" so they can capture, sample and analyze the data essential to their own grand challenges.**

CONNECTED HEALTHCARE

The healthcare industry is experiencing a sea change in data proliferation as medical records become computerized and more medical and personal computing devices record, store and transmit data. Analyzing large data sets will be increasingly important for population health (e.g., disease surveillance, provider comparisons, post-marketing drug surveillance) as well as personalized healthcare.[19]

To that end, a global healthcare ecosystem will emerge marked by a rich pool of data to support connected care and by research collaborations for advancing diagnoses, treatments and outcomes. Signs of the ecosystem include progress in electronic health records, more connected health data, and advances in health informatics and health information exchanges. The vision is a grand healthcare platform of information – a network of networks connecting patients, providers, researchers, insurers and health agencies.

> **The vision is a grand healthcare platform of information – a network of networks connecting patients, providers, researchers, insurers and health agencies.**

One step towards this meshing of networks is the European Institute for Health Records (EuroRec), which is promoting the use of high-quality electronic health records (EHRs) in Europe through a federation of existing national health centers.[20] By defining quality criteria, EuroRec supports certification. EuroRec is working to consolidate the different approaches to EHR certification into a common set of criteria, available in all European languages. These quality criteria are being validated and tested in member countries through an ongoing project, EHR-Q^TN. (See Figure 5.) The objective is to harmonize EHR certification across Europe, an important step towards product harmonization and the big payoff: data interoperability.

Figure 5 The European Institute for Health Records (EuroRec) is promoting high-quality electronic health records in Europe through a federation of national health centers. Its EHR-Q project focuses on quality criteria and certification of EHR systems.

Source: EuroRec

As work progresses to connect networks broadly, there is immediate value in simply connecting healthcare data. One example of this is PRISM, the Post-Licensure Rapid Immunization Safety Monitoring system. This system, designed for the U.S. Food and Drug Administration by CSC, helps ensure population health by monitoring vaccine safety. PRISM was designed to monitor the safety of the H1N1 (swine flu) vaccine in the United States during the 2009 flu pandemic. PRISM monitored over 35 million people, assembling data from five national payer databases, linked with immunization registry data from nine states, and ultimately tracking over three million doses. This was approximately twice as many doses and four times as many people as past initiatives. PRISM, a 2011 CSC Chairman's Award for Excellence finalist, mines large amounts of disparate data, quickly, to avert potential

health disasters. Its techniques are being used today to monitor other vaccines and medications.

Back in the clinician's office, one critical challenge to connecting data is that most useful clinical data is still captured as text. What is needed is a natural language search engine, such as the University of Michigan Health System's Electronic Medical Record Search Engine (EMERSE), that includes computational learning and sophisticated algorithms to draw meaningful conclusions from the data.[21] Right now human review is needed to separate the wheat from the chaff. Beyond that, health information exchanges are needed to integrate and share the data – patient data, clinical data and insurance data – regionally, nationally and globally (the global healthcare ecosystem). As care crosses boundaries, so too must the data, which will be aggregated to detect trends, patterns, similarities and key differences, leading to faster and more effective disease management.

FINANCIAL SERVICES DATA DIVES DEEPER

Data has been, and will continue to be, the main ingredient in financial services. But today the data goes deeper – there is more of it, from more sources – and demands more analysis to deliver new levels of competitiveness.

> Data has been, and will continue to be, the main ingredient in financial services. But today the data goes deeper – there is more of it, from more sources – and demands more analysis to deliver new levels of competitiveness.

In financial services, the name of the game is risk, its consequences for the allocation of capital, and how to minimize it while maximizing return on capital and maintaining regulatory compliance. Risk is represented by consumers, investments and markets; having data about all, from point-of-sale (purchase) to mandated monitoring, requires assembling and assessing data from across the financial industry spectrum. The spectacular growth in data sources can provide greater insight if filtered and aggregated by serious analytics; otherwise, financial services providers face an ocean of data without context.

Retail banks are focusing analytical resources on three areas: credit worthiness and monitoring, profitability per customer, and product testing and monitoring. They are seeking better analytics to determine how to distinguish good from bad loans, how to identify signs of delinquency, and – most significantly – what to do to prevent delinquency (e.g., modify the existing loan, work out a payment plan).

Determining individual customer profitability requires the ability to leverage all enterprise data about a customer to determine his or her overall profit contribution to the bank. The more profitable customer receives better rates, higher rewards, forgiveness for late payments, and flexible options should a collection situation arise. To accomplish this, not only does the bank need the analytics and the data, but it may also have to change business processes and organization structure to more adeptly use the data (for example, combine deposit and credit card divisions, as Bank of America has done[22]).

Product testing and monitoring are key to the future. Banks must balance fees, interest rates, rewards and incentives for good (profitable) customer behavior. The ability to quickly model products, take them to market, and monitor and track the resulting profitability will be essential for banks to maintain and grow profitable credit card, prepaid card, debit card, home equity loan and other products. In addition, customer segmentation is back. Smart companies are learning exactly what customers value and are delivering – PNC's Virtual Wallet is an example. Companies are balancing risk, growth and cost, with data management as a key enabler.

On the trading floor, investors are turning more and more to data and computers to make trading decisions for them. A new crop of companies is harnessing machine learning for investing, with good results; one hedge fund company, Rebellion Research, has beat the S&P 500 by an average of 10 percent a year from 2007, when it began trading, through mid-2010.[23] Rebellion Research's program, called Star, processes enormous amounts of data quickly, "learns" what works, and can adjust its stock-picking strategy on the fly, unlike the typical quant approach, which is not as flexible or dynamic.[24] Star "monitors about 30 factors that can affect a stock's performance, such as price-to-earnings ratios or interest rates. The program regularly crunches more than a

decade of historical market data and the latest market action to size up whether to buy or sell a stock."[25]

Off the trading floor and inside the data center, it's all about transaction speed. Here physical distance counts. No one wants to be late for a transaction and miss an opportunity because of limits set by the speed of light. Just as having a seat on the stock exchange affords certain advantages, the future might see that rack position in the data center creates speed advantages between trading partners as data is moving from node to node. Indeed, a veritable "arms race" in the data center is brewing; new rules are being considered for colocation services for high-frequency trading to ensure equal access.[26]

For insurance companies, data has always fueled the actuarial coffers for pricing, risk selection and driving probability of profit to a fine science. But the coffers have overflowed due to slow adoption of technology that takes advantage of analytics. Just as property and casualty insurers ride on the leading edge using demographic and company data to make the best possible risk selection decisions, along comes social media adding a new layer of complexity and depth to risk insight. As with banks and other financial institutions, insurance companies will have to meet the data challenge to reach and keep the right customers to stay competitive in their marketplace.

MARKETING: MORE PRECISE, MORE MOBILE, MORE SOCIAL

Marketing is becoming more precise and more comprehensive as analytics take hold. Trident Marketing runs its business on advanced analytics to deliver profitable marketing campaigns, both digital and traditional, by better targeting its customers with ads.[27] Trident has three subsidiaries: Direct Sat TV, a national marketing and sales organization for DIRECTV; Advanced Direct Security, a national marketing partner for ADT Security Services; and Travel Resorts of America, which owns and markets two high-end RV resorts. Through its marketing campaigns, Trident needs to

> **Marketing is becoming more precise and more comprehensive as analytics take hold.**

deliver the maximum number of paying customers for each business. Its call center handles four million calls per year.

By using analytics that take into account thousands of factors culled from Web search data, Trident's telemarketers know exactly whom to call at what moment in what geography about what product. The analytics have provided a better insight into customer yield, improving overall results by including churn predictions and customer acquisition predictions. (Results are typically measured as cost per acquisition after churn.)

In the digital realm, when Trident introduced paid search analytics for sales occurring on the Web or in its call center, the cost of sales dropped by 50 percent and, simultaneously, sales volume increased by 10 percent within 60 days. Trident did this by analyzing a small population of Internet viewers with known demographic attributes, and then using pattern recognition to analyze a very large data set of Web surfing behavior and define demographic groups within the data set. People in each demographic group were then served the optimal ad on each Web page they viewed.

In addition, by more accurately predicting customer churn, Trident was able to lower its financial reserves and therefore working capital requirements by 10 percent. In the Direct Sat TV sales department, adding analytics-enabled sales management helped increase revenue per call by 10 percent from selling additional products. Looking ahead, Trident plans to use automated scripting analytics to improve real-time interactions while agents are on calls with customers.

InsightExpress helps advertisers, media agencies, Web publishers and marketers optimize their marketing initiatives across online, mobile and other media. Such initiatives generate huge amounts of data, which InsightExpress captures and analyzes. The company focuses on message evaluation, advertising effectiveness and creative development using powerful analytics to dissect data rapidly and discern detailed behavior patterns.

The company captures over a billion ad impressions a month, running analytics against the data to understand events such as "person A saw ad B on site C at time D" or questions like "What is the intent to purchase among women 18-34 in households earning over $100,000?" For that type of question, the analytics engine "must filter out the relevant sample from the broader population, determine that it has a valid sample size,

evaluate the sample against 2,000 different studies, and then determine an average to get the number the client is looking for."[28] InsightExpress can run such queries in seconds rather than minutes using advanced analytics.

The company has made a major investment in analytics in order to respond to its customers with speed, precision and flexibility. As TV and Internet blur, as magazines and Internet blur, and as mobility comes on strong, InsightExpress needs to be able to grow and change with the market and its rapidly changing data.

Social networks are a potential gold mine for marketing, and businesses are challenged to put that data to use. This is data that did not exist 10 years ago: opinions, comments, relationships, work histories, personal and professional interests, and other tidbits.

This is data people value. Consider the very successful initial public offering of LinkedIn, valued at $4.3 billion at its May 2011 IPO.[29] This was the first IPO of the social networks. Founded in 2003, LinkedIn has roughly 119 million members representing over 200 countries (leading countries are the United States, India and the United Kingdom).[30] The company reinvented professional networking by linking data and people in wholly new ways to find, and recruit for, jobs. LinkedIn provides computationally intensive services like People You May Know, Viewers of This Profile Also Viewed, and much of its job-matching functionality. The company uses complex algorithms that draw on data from up to dozens of sources.[31]

At Twitter, founded in 2006 and valued in July 2011 at a whopping $7 billion,[32] the focus on analytics has been tools for the person using Twitter. Twitter boasts over 160 million members who send an average of 155 million tweets per day.[33] Numerous analytics tools have been popping up to get a handle on such things as a member's popularity and clout (TwitterGrader), number of tweets sent (TweetStats) and general trends (Trendistic).[34] Twitter trends shed important light on the unrest in the Middle East and North Africa in early 2011.

The Data rEvolution impacts all industries. Organizations have great expectations to do more with more data. At a business level, the Data rEvolution is igniting collaboration, innovation, new business processes and speed. At a data processing level, it is demanding new technologies and techniques. Let's look at these next.

A CHANGING FOUNDATION:
NEW METHODS TO MANAGE BIG DATA

The Data rEvolution is boosting the volume and diversity of information, shortening processing time, and demanding more advanced analytics. These demands are driving radical shifts in how we build infrastructures to deal with data. Designers are experimenting and pushing beyond their comfort zones. Today we see petabytes of data distributed across thousands of commodity machines that are processing the data in parallel. This type of "shared nothing" architecture represents an entirely new way for enterprises to store, process and manage information. The foundation for our data is changing.

Big Internet companies are fueling this change. Recently, the core components of specialized shared nothing software solutions from the likes of Google and Amazon have been abstracted into a form that can be more generally applied to other industries. This chapter focuses on how we can combine these new software abstractions in data and application domains to build the data foundation of the future. We will examine shared nothing architecture; distributed processing frameworks, which demonstrate shared nothing architecture; and non-relational and parallel relational databases, the new faces in a shared nothing world. The days of the "one size fits all" relational database built on shared disk/memory architecture are over.

SHARED NOTHING

How is it that Google responds in milliseconds to queries that search the Internet while most people complain vigorously about their company's internal applications? Answer: Google has invented a new way. Enterprises like Google are distributing the data and performing massively parallel processing for faster results, using "shared nothing" architectures in which each computing node is self-contained (in contrast to a "shared disk/memory" architecture in which nodes are dependent on, say, a central data store). The convergence of distributed hardware, data and application approaches has led this foundational shift, as illustrated in Figure 6.

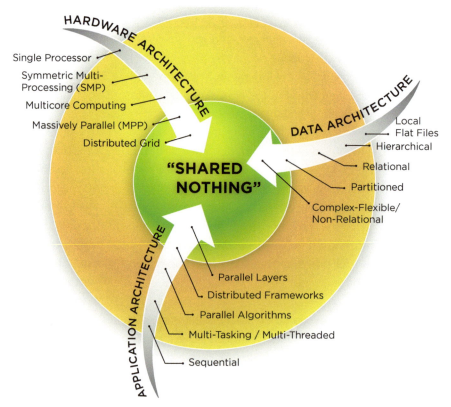

Figure 6 The convergence of hardware, application and data architectures to a stateless "shared nothing" world is redefining the data foundation.

Source: CSC

The term "shared nothing" was coined in the mid 1980s by database luminary Michael Stonebraker in the context of multi-processor systems.[35] The underlying principle behind shared nothing architecture is simple, yet can be challenging to adhere to: if tasks and data can be divided up and distributed to team members to work on independently, then the overhead of coordinating and synchronizing access to shared infrastructure among team members can be removed. In complex systems with many members or nodes working together, this overhead can quickly become unmanageable. By removing this overhead, we can start building massively scalable systems to handle large processing loads.

Cut to the late 1990s and early 2000s. Moore's and Metcalfe's laws manifested themselves in powerful multi-processor and multicore computers connected together via faster and reliable networks. Enterprises now have access to large-scale distributed grids, also available in cloud form. Following this next phase of shared nothing hardware architecture, the accompanying evolution of application architectures occurred. This was first evident in distributed community research projects such as distributed.net and SETI@home,[36] and then in commercial environments such as those of Google and Amazon, who began using shared nothing application architectures to support their distributed Web applications.

Our understanding of data architecture has also matured. We are learning how to partition and denormalize data for effective shared nothing processing. In addition, the explosion of unstructured data and complex structured data (e.g., documents and graphs) has meant a rethink about the suitability of relational databases for everything; this is the crux of the recent non-relational database movement embraced by many Web start-up companies.

DISTRIBUTED PROCESSING FRAMEWORKS: DIVIDE AND CONQUER

One of the more exciting characteristics of new data processing systems is their ability to spread the data across an unusually large number of processing nodes. In the traditional relational world, such massive horizontal distribution is difficult at best. But now it is entirely possible to call upon a large grid (or cloud) of commodity computers to process data. The days of buying bigger, faster, expensive machines to scale up processing power have given way to acquiring (via outright purchase or pay-per-use) large numbers of inexpensive machines networked together into a cooperative grid of processors. Indeed, this distributed approach may be the *only* way to meet the computing needs of today's complex, data-rich problems. A problem that may have taken hours or days to process can now be analyzed in minutes or seconds.[37]

Another benefit of this grid processing approach is the ability to scale up and down as required. Enterprises can allocate minimal resources during quiet periods and add more for peak periods – i.e., the cloud computing model. Using a hybrid cloud model, enterprises can even "burst"

> **This distributed approach may be the *only* way to meet the computing needs of today's complex, data-rich problems.**

their private infrastructure processing onto public cloud infrastructure like Amazon.

The new challenge becomes how to get a massive grid of processors to work together cooperatively, yet independently, to comb through large amounts of data and produce meaningful results. That's where the distributed processing framework comes in. The framework is designed to manage and distribute the data across the machines, send application instructions out to all the networked computers to work on in parallel, coordinate and collect the individual results, and assemble and produce a final result. Processing is pushed out to individual nodes where the data resides, instead of the traditional approach in which data is retrieved from all nodes and processed on a few central computers. Such "in-database" techniques are moving to the fore.

Harnessing MapReduce and Hadoop. The most well-known distributed processing framework is MapReduce, patented by Google.[38] MapReduce simplifies processing of massive data sets and gives programmers a common mechanism to define and orchestrate a complex processing task that is distributed across a large cluster of computers (in Google's case, tens of thousands of inexpensive computing nodes[39]). Many companies today leverage MapReduce principles for ingesting enormous amounts of data for analysis.

Google applies MapReduce to all the complex unstructured data it gathers from the Internet. Google runs thousands of MapReduce jobs each day to provide up-to-date query results.[40] How Google orchestrates these jobs is some of the secret sauce behind what makes Google work. The company's brilliance provides millions of people each day with a way to see sub-second responses to queries because Google has figured out how to "MapReduce" the Internet's content prior to your query.

Seeing the obvious gains that MapReduce has delivered, many enterprises are taking advantage of MapReduce by using the Hadoop open source technology stack, which includes an open source implementation of MapReduce, the Hadoop Distributed File System (HDFS) and the HBase non-relational column-family database.[41] Yahoo has made Hadoop a cornerstone of its operations and is the largest contributor in the Hadoop community.[42] Hadoop users include LinkedIn, Facebook, eHarmony, Quantcast and Rackspace.

Online matchmaker eHarmony uses Hadoop to make recommendations about matches for its customers. All the matches, scores (used to rate a person's attributes) and member information must be archived daily. The company needs the power of Hadoop to handle increasingly complex matching models. eHarmony has more than 20 million registered members and processes active profiles daily, analyzing 29 different attributes per profile.[43]

Quantcast focuses on audience data. Quantcast provides an audience measurement and predictive analytics service to marketing agencies and media publishers so they can target online advertisements to individuals. Quantcast measures everyone directly rather than taking samples, which has been the traditional (pre-Internet) approach to audience measurement. The company uses a Hadoop cluster to analyze over 300 billion events (cookies) per month from 1.2 billion people on the Internet, equating to processing 1.5 petabytes of data every day. These numbers increase daily; the horizontal scalability of Hadoop allows Quantcast to add more nodes to the cluster as needed.[44]

Rackspace, which provides enterprise hosting services, uses Hadoop to query terabytes of log data from its hosted email service.[45] Prior to Hadoop, engineers had to log in to individual servers and examine email logs manually to troubleshoot customer problems. As the company grew to over a dozen mail servers, this approach became unworkable. Hadoop provided a scalable solution that was fast and reliable, and that indexed the data so that it could be searched efficiently. Data is now indexed every 10 minutes and is available to customer care representatives in about 15 minutes, so customer issues can be addressed quickly and engineers can stay focused on product development. Rackspace reminds us that the opportunities are endless; just replace log data with call center data, clickstream data or social network data.

Hadoop adoption by commercial and government organizations is not a matter of "if" but "when." Cost will likely be a motivator, especially when the cost of traditional analytics is deemed too high compared to new methods. For example, one of our UK customers is leveraging Hadoop to run what had been a conventional online analytical processing (OLAP) application, reducing a 17-hour job to five hours, at less than *one-tenth* the cost. The application was rewritten as a MapReduce job and applied against the same data on a 50-node Hadoop cluster running on Dell x86 servers.

> **Hadoop adoption by commercial and government organizations is not a matter of "if" but "when."**

In addition to being faster and cheaper, Hadoop offers other benefits:[46]

- try and retry – "fail fast" promotes rapid experimentation and innovation

- no formal data modeling required in advance – grab your data, put it into a simple model, and add what you need when you need it using a schema-less design

- not necessary to "know where you're going" in advance – programs written in Hadoop can find data relationships in data of any structure

MapReduce/Hadoop Innovations Go Commercial.

Although Google is credited with pioneering the MapReduce framework and inspiring the open source community to bring it into the mainstream, many commercial players are getting into the game.

Cloudera distributes a commercial version of Hadoop much the way Red Hat and others distribute Linux. Cloudera's Distribution including Apache Hadoop, or CDH, offers its own utilities and unique extensions to Hadoop, bringing more value and completeness to the technology stack. eBay uses CDH to improve its search results for items, using a ranking function that takes into account multiple factors like price, listing format, seller track performance and relevance, with the ability to add new factors to test hypotheses.[47]

Following Cloudera, other major data processing and storage vendors have released commercial versions of Hadoop, including EMC with Greenplum HD and IBM with InfoSphere BigInsights. Yahoo's Hortonworks spinoff will develop and maintain Apache Hadoop, provide enterprise support, and may offer additions for paying customers.[48] Another startup, MapR Technologies, has also released its own Hadoop distribution that includes a number of Hadoop tools and enhancements that improve performance and fault-tolerance of the underlying framework. EMC has licensed parts of MapR's commercial distribution for integration into the enterprise version of Greenplum HD.[49]

Informatica and Cloudera are developing a connector, giving the many developers who already use Informatica's integration platform an on-ramp to Hadoop processing.[50] A new offering from start-up Hadapt, scheduled for release in 2011, combines relational techniques with Hadoop to process both structured and unstructured data. The company's Adaptive Query Execution technology splits analytic workloads dynamically between relational databases and Hadoop to optimize performance, and is designed specifically for cloud analytics.[51]

Karmasphere provides software for business analysts and developers to work with data in Hadoop clusters. The software enables enterprises to work with Hadoop data using familiar tools like SQL.[52] (SQL is the database access tool of choice in the corporate world, whereas Hadoop's main access tool is MapReduce.)

Karmasphere's partnership with Teradata, announced in October 2010, unites two massively parallel data environments so companies can run highly distributed MapReduce jobs accessing data from Hadoop files (unstructured) and Teradata databases (structured). The idea is to have "an easy-to-use on-ramp to Big Data."[53] Teradata's acquisitions of Aprimo in December 2010 and Aster Data in April 2011 reinforce the company's commitment to big data analytics.[54]

Intellicus Technologies also provides an on-ramp to Hadoop from the enterprise, having announced that its business intelligence product will support Hadoop via Hive

and Aster Data.[55] The application can schedule MapReduce tasks to run on Hadoop to feed its dashboards and reports.

Another commercialization of MapReduce comes from Splunk, which applies MapReduce to machine-generated corporate IT data. The company has created a distributed search, indexing and analysis application for IT data such as audit, server and application logs. The challenges of setting up the infrastructure, getting data into the distributed database, and writing MapReduce programs are handled by Splunk's installation and configuration process, freeing people to focus on using the product for its intended purpose – proactive monitoring of distributed IT systems.

Splunk uses its own search engine language to look across any data in any format to help find security breaches and anomalies. It can answer rich search queries to pinpoint activities of interest, such as a particular person with a particular job description is generating a greater-than-20-percent deviation in email traffic on a Wednesday afternoon. Or, it can ferret out insider abuse by monitoring internal IP address activity, seeing that an insider has accessed a customer account and changed information in it, and matching that person's username to his active directory ID, which links to his employee badge data that shows when the employee swiped his badge to enter and later leave the data center. "We can monitor this person's activity. We know his role, title and phone number. We can see him copy the customer data to a flash drive and then leave the data center. We've got him – we can issue an alert," explains Tim Young, cyber security expert, Splunk. "We've got evidence in the data from watching everything he does in real time."

Splunk has a pre-built module to support stringent Federal Information Security Management Act (FISMA) continuous monitoring requirements, which dictate that U.S. government agencies and their contractors must continuously track security controls in order to preemptively identify and remediate security risks. Using a distributed and parallel processing architecture, Splunk can consolidate, index and correlate logs and events from all relevant systems in near real time, beyond the capabilities of standard security information and event management (SIEM) tools. For example, the module can automatically report when a terminated employee uses a laptop that has not been returned, or when attempts have been made to modify audit trail data. This information is presented in high-level dashboards for status monitoring and in detailed analysis reports for ongoing assessment of security controls.[56]

HADOOP TOOLS

Several tools have been created to help developers build multi-layered complex Hadoop applications. Pig and Cascading are early examples of tools designed to help developers express parallel applications on large data sets leveraging an underlying distributed processing framework such as MapReduce without having to think in "MapReduce" terms.[57] These technologies pave the way for more parallelization in the enterprise to tackle vast quantities of data and yield new insights.

We are in the early days of seeing new architectures spring up leveraging these exciting tools. While the choices are many, a complete technology stack in the parallel distributed database world of the future might look something like the Hadoop stack in Figure 7.

Tools like these, along with others, can be acquired from the open source Apache foundation or through integrated commercial packages. It is a rapidly evolving world of tools, many only in the early stages, yet it is only a matter of time before production-ready instances will be available for general distribution.

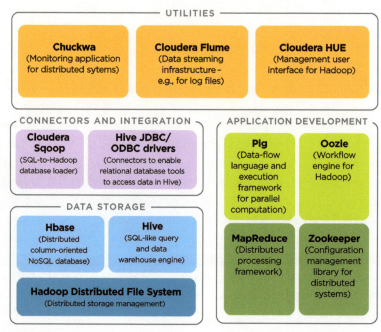

Figure 7 SAMPLE PARALLEL DISTRIBUTED STACK BASED ON HADOOP TECHNOLOGIES

UTILITIES

Chuckwa (Monitoring application for distributed sytems)

Cloudera Flume (Data streaming infrastructure – e.g., for log files)

Cloudera HUE (Management user interface for Hadoop)

CONNECTORS AND INTEGRATION

Cloudera Sqoop (SQL-to-Hadoop database loader)

Hive JDBC/ODBC drivers (Connectors to enable relational database tools to access data in Hive)

DATA STORAGE

Hbase (Distributed column-oriented NoSQL database)

Hive (SQL-like query and data warehouse engine)

Hadoop Distributed File System (Distributed storage management)

APPLICATION DEVELOPMENT

Pig (Data-flow language and execution framework for parallel computation)

Oozie (Workflow engine for Hadoop)

MapReduce (Distributed processing framework)

Zookeeper (Configuration management library for distributed systems)

Source: CSC

NetApp is also making a move towards Hadoop with its announcement of Hadoop-optimized storage appliances. Its Hadoop Open Storage System, based on Engenio technologies recently acquired from LSI Corporation, are designed for storage-centric, and mixed storage and compute-centric, Hadoop applications. Unlike other vendors, NetApp is not attempting to build another Hadoop distribution; its focus is on supporting open source Hadoop with high-performance and fault-tolerant access to external disk arrays, which can be easily expanded as data volumes grow.[58]

Outside the Hadoop realm, Microsoft Research has created a generic distributed processing framework called Dryad.

Dryad allows developers to build large-scale data-parallel programs simply by writing a series of small sequential programs with any number of inputs and outputs, and then creating a graph of these programs by linking their inputs and outputs together to achieve the required results. The Dryad engine is capable of taking this graph and automatically parallelizing and managing the execution of the programs over multiple processor cores and nodes. In many cases, the graph itself is automatically generated if developers use higher-level abstractions such as DryadLINQ (an extension of Microsoft LINQ technology that integrates database queries into .NET programs).

In contrast, MapReduce restricts developers to only two types of operations, map and reduce, and these limit the number of inputs and outputs at each stage (though not the size of each input – i.e., number of input files).

Dryad is currently being used to run Bing, with DryadLINQ available for academic use. Given Dryad's generic nature, it could become much more popular in the future, especially if it is not limited to Microsoft platforms.

Yahoo has also created a generic distributed processing framework called S4. The technology is different than MapReduce and Dryad in that S4 is designed for real-time stream processing instead of batch. Yahoo has open-sourced the framework, allowing the broader community to drive future development.[59]

UNDERLYING DATABASE: NON-RELATIONAL PLAYS BIG

To handle the complexity and flexibility inherent in the new world of diverse data, the database is shifting from relational to non-relational. This is a revolutionary change, for the relational model has been the dominant method of database design since it was introduced *40 years ago*. In the world of IT, where change is extraordinarily rapid, 40 years is an eternity; companies like Google are recognizing the need for change and are redefining the rules.

The interest in non-relational models is being fueled, in part, by the surge in unstructured data, shown in Figure 8. Unstructured data is less rigid, less ordered and more inter-related. (Sources of this unstructured data tsunami include Web applications, social networks, video and still cameras, and sensor networks.) This is in stark contrast to traditional relational database models, which are highly structured, normalized and densely populated. The chaotic world of unstructured data does not fit into the orderly world of structured data. New places to store, process and analyze the unstructured data – often combined with structure data – are needed.

The new breed of non-relational database designs is built to scale for the complexities of the unstructured world and is network oriented, semi-structured and sparsely populated. Ironically, in many ways the non-relational databases attempt to store data more simply, with fewer dependencies, fewer constraints and fewer assumptions. The intent is to not force structure on the data but to let the data reveal structure as it is examined from various points of view.

WORLDWIDE FILE-BASED VERSUS BLOCK-BASED STORAGE CAPACITY SHIPMENTS, 2009–2014

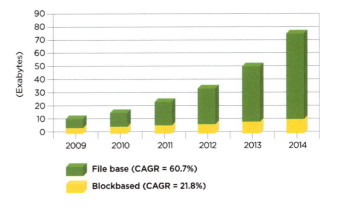

Figure 8 Unstructured data (file-based) has become the predominant data type and is growing far faster than transactional (block-based) data. The surge in unstructured data is a key driver of non-relational databases.

Source: IDC, Worldwide File-Based Storage 2010–2014 Forecast: Consolidation, Efficiency, and Objects Shape Market, #223558

And, the intent is to store this data "forever" – there is no reason to delete given cheap, scalable storage.

The Rise of Not Only SQL. Today there are a variety of options in database design that reflect the growing need for a new kind of database that deviates from some of the fundamental characteristics of traditional relational databases. A movement dubbed "NoSQL" (Not Only SQL)[60] calls attention to this new breed of databases that generally do not require fixed table schemas, usually avoid join operations, and typically are designed to scale horizontally across many processing nodes – features that are most definitely non-relational. Numerous solutions exist today; it can get quite confusing as you begin to explore and evaluate.

To help make sense of it, Figure 9 describes both relational and non-relational databases. Note that many non-relational solutions are from start-ups; some are open source sub-projects[61] under the well-known Apache project (e.g., HBase and Cassandra) and are backed by the likes of Google and Yahoo.[62] Market demand and computing pressures will determine which solutions survive and which design philosophies endure. Amazon has demonstrated the power behind key-value databases,[63] Google and Yahoo both utilize gigantic column databases,[64] and Facebook has proven the power of the social graph.[65]

Figure 9 RELATIONAL AND NON-RELATIONAL DATABASES

DESIGN APPROACH	DESCRIPTION	EXAMPLES	WHEN TO USE
RELATIONAL DATABASES			
Traditional Relational Database	Traditional database that stores its information as a collection of two-dimensional tables (relations) made up of rows (tuples) and columns (attributes) that can be joined by using common data elements in one or more columns.	Oracle, SQL Server, DB2, Informix, Sybase, MySQL, PostgreSQL	In many cases, traditional relational databases are still appropriate to use for transaction processing and basic analysis applications because they are more mature, well understood and can be adapted to fit many scenarios. High performance traditional relational databases such as Oracle Exadata are available if more power is required.
Parallel Relational Database	A relational database that is distributed across many processing nodes, allowing parallel execution of queries (both traditional SQL and new distributed processing queries).	Teradata/Aster Data, Netezza, Greenplum, VoltDB	Many parallel relational databases are targeted at batch and near-real-time analytics applications that operate on large volumes of tabular structured data. Some support real-time online transaction processing too. These databases can also serve as rapid prototyping testbeds for developing algorithms to run on large distributed processing systems like Hadoop.
Column-Oriented Relational Database	A relational database that stores its content by columns rather than by rows. However, it still looks like a traditional relational data model and typically supports standard SQL queries.	Vertica, Sybase IQ, SAND, Kickfire	Column-oriented relational databases are suitable for read-intensive analytics applications such as data warehouses, from which aggregation-type reports are generated (e.g., monthly balance of debit and credit transactions for accounts). Aggregation of columnar data is very fast because data in a column is stored together.
NOSQL DATABASES			
Key-Value Databases	A database model that stores values indexed by a key built on either a hash data structure or a tree data structure like a b-tree. Data values are grouped-together entities based on the key, and atomic operations can be mapped to individual entities.	Amazon SimpleDB, Chordless, Redis, Riak, Scalaris, Tokyo Cabinet/Tyrant, GT.M, Scalien, BerkeleyDB, MemcacheDB, HamsterDB, NorthScale, Mnesia, LightCloud, Amazon Dynamo, Voldemort, Dynomite, M/DB, PNUTS/Sherpa	Key-value stores are suitable for high-performance Web application caches and online transaction processing when horizontal scalability is required and the application data model is simple (e.g., shopping carts on e-commerce sites).

Figure 9 RELATIONAL AND NON-RELATIONAL DATABASES *(continued)*

DESIGN APPROACH	DESCRIPTION	EXAMPLES	WHEN TO USE
NOSQL DATABASES, (continued)			
Column-Family Databases	Extension of key-value databases that supports a flexible number of fields ("columns") for each key.	HBase, Cassandra, Hypertable, BigTable, KAI	Column databases should be considered for high-performance and horizontally scalable online transaction processing when the application data model is more complex than simple key-value structures. They may also be suitable for some real-time analytics applications where data is accumulated over time (e.g., server farm statistics).
Document Databases	A database model that stores information such that each record is a document that has certain characteristics. Any number of fields of any length can be added to a document. Fields can also contain multiple pieces of data.	CouchDB, MongoDB, RavenDB, Terrastore, Jackrabbit, IBM Lotus/Domino	Document databases are ideal for online transaction processing and analytic applications when the data is hierarchical in nature (e.g., Web blogs). This can be challenging to map to and access from a relational data model.
Graph Databases	A database model that uses nodes, edges and properties to represent and store information. The entity being connected is not a record but an object, such as a person "Bob." A graph database allows you to easily see all the connections to Bob.	Neo4j, Sones, InfoGrid, HyperGraphDB, AllegroGraph, VertexDB, DEX, FlockDB	Graph databases should be considered when transaction processing and analytic applications store and analyze highly complex data with inter-related entities, such as social networks or graph-based scientific data.
OTHER DATABASES			
Object Database	A database model in which information is represented in the form of objects as used in object-oriented programming. Many object databases retain standard relational database features such as queries and transactions, and avoid performance and development issues associated with mapping objects to a relational model.	db4o, Versant, Objectivity, Matisse, Perst, OrientDB, KiokuDB, Gemfire	These databases are suitable when your online transaction processing application needs high-performance data access on an object-oriented data model.

Many organizations, ranging from start-ups to well-established companies and research organizations, are investigating and actively using NoSQL. Foursquare, a popular location-based service, uses MongoDB for member "check-ins" and to answer "who's here?" queries.[66] Intuit, the creator of small business solutions such as Quicken, also uses MongoDB but for tracking member activities across its Web sites.[67] Mozilla uses Riak to store data from Test Pilot, a component of its popular browser product that records errors people encounter.[68] CERN uses a combination of CouchDB and MongoDB to store and process scientific measurements from the Large Hadron Collider.[69]

Although many NoSQL database products began as open source projects, enterprise versions of these databases with commercial support are emerging. For example, MongoDB is supported by 10gen, CouchDB products are available from Couchbase and Cloudant, and Neo Technology has released an enterprise edition of the Neo4j graph database.

That said, non-relational databases are not the "silver bullet" that will solve all database computing problems. Non-relational databases may not be for you if your data has to pass the ACID test (atomicity, consistency, isolation, durability).[70] But if your data is unstructured and highly interrelated, non-relational may be a good fit. The technology is maturing rapidly, with many solutions in testing.

Remember Relational. Given that non-relational databases are not a silver bullet, it is important to remember that relational databases are not going away. At over $20 billion in sales in 2010 and growing,[71] relational databases and their supporting hardware, software, management and maintenance solutions are not broken and are not likely to be mothballed anytime soon.[72] In fact, the continuing evolution of relational technologies is following two paths: parallel and cloud. New parallel relational solutions offer significantly faster processing speeds and horizontal scaling across many nodes. (We will get to these.)

Relational models are being moved off premise to the cloud. Database as a Service (DaaS) is a phenomenon just starting; have your database in the cloud and wrap application services around it. Database.com (from Salesforce.com) is a pioneer, initially open to developers in 2010 and offering a full developer preview in 2011.[73] This is the same database technology and infrastructure that power Salesforce.com.[74] DaaS directly feeds a new era of experimentation and participation as data is made readily available as a service, not

> DaaS directly feeds a new era of experimentation and participation as data is made readily available as a service, not hoarded in a proprietary, walled-in database. It is also the next logical step in the evolution of cloud computing.

hoarded in a proprietary, walled-in database. It is also the next logical step in the evolution of cloud computing.[75]

PARALLEL RELATIONAL PLATFORMS FOR ANALYTICS

The urgency to process and analyze all the data flowing in, both structured and unstructured, has put renewed focus on parallel computing, particularly parallel relational platforms. Parallel relational engines can easily reach 100 times the speed of their predecessors. These significant performance improvements can be achieved while retaining the familiar relational data model, ad-hoc SQL queries and integration with existing analytics tools such as SAS. This makes parallel relational platforms more enticing to enterprises.

Many parallel relational database vendors are also incorporating the new distributed processing frameworks. Many already had an eye towards distributed architectures and are now moving ahead full force, in some respects responding to the NoSQL movement. For example, Aster Data (Teradata), Greenplum (EMC) and Netezza (IBM) all support MapReduce, should the enterprise want to process its data in this manner as opposed to using SQL. Aster Data coined the term SQL-MapReduce for its innovative, patented method for integrating SQL and MapReduce on its platform.

These analytic platforms can process staggering amounts of data. A major stock exchange uses Greenplum as part of its fraud detection system. Every minute during a trading day, large volumes of trade latency data are loaded into Greenplum and then analyzed for suspicious activity using a series of functions (written using SQL). Analysts are then notified in real time if any unusual activity has been detected. All of this data load and analysis must be completed before the next minute.[76] A major online gambling site uses Aster

Data's analytics to detect fraud in near real time, analyzing virtual hands of poker every 15 minutes instead of the previous weekly method, processing some 140,000 hands per second versus 1,200 in the past.[77] Parallelizing the analytic logic, which was previously run on a stand-alone application server, directly in the Aster Data analytic platform provided the speed needed to sift through terabytes of data on an ongoing basis for fast fraud detection. InsightExpress

uses Aster Data to analyze over a billion ad impressions, captured monthly, in seconds rather than minutes. (See the Great Expectations chapter.) Aster Data provides the necessary speed and scalability.

Not surprisingly, players in the parallel relational market are taking different architectural approaches. Teradata was the first large-scale parallel relational database built

IMPROVING DATA PROCESSING PERFORMANCE USING SOLID-STATE DRIVES AND IN-MEMORY STORAGE

A major contributor to data processing performance is access time to the data. In recent times, we have seen the cost of solid-state drives (SSDs) drop as their capacities have increased. These high-speed storage devices are now large enough to hold a significant portion of data sets, thereby providing a relatively easy way to boost processing performance over systems that primarily use hard disks. Oracle has integrated SSDs into its Exadata platform for this reason.[78] Another example is AOL, which built a 50-terabyte storage area network (SAN) using SSDs that has delivered a four-fold improvement in relational database throughput.[79] Acunu, a big data start-up, is optimizing database and operating system software to use SSDs on commodity hardware, claiming an order of magnitude or more performance improvement.[80] So far, Cassandra has been ported, with work being performed on Hadoop, Voldemort and memcached.[81] The hard disk is becoming the next tape drive, used only for archiving data.

Memory remains the fastest storage medium available. Platforms are emerging that take advantage of large memory capacities now available in computers. SAP recently announced HANA (High Performance Analytics Appliance), a scalable, in-memory appliance that combines SAP's in-memory computing and database platforms. Data is stored and processed in a combination of memory-backed traditional and column-oriented relational databases. Persistent storage such as SSD is only used to ensure data is durable and can be recovered in the event of a computer restart.[82]

Some database products have taken a more extreme approach: Why not store all data in-memory across many distributed nodes? Such a distributed system uses shared nothing architecture, so data storage and processing can be performed virtually independently between nodes in parallel, forming a data grid. Data is replicated across a number of nodes to ensure durability in case of a node failure.

This approach has been used for real-time online transaction processing where low-latency access and throughput is of paramount importance. VMware GemFire, a non-relational in-memory data grid product, has been deployed at a number of financial services companies, including JPMorgan Chase, where it is used to perform real-time pricing and risk calculations for traders. With this data grid, calculations are running two orders of magnitude faster, with pricing performance calculations completed every 45 seconds instead of every 45 minutes.[83] Data grids are not restricted to non-relational systems; VoltDB has applied the same in-memory shared nothing architecture to the relational data model.[84]

As the need for faster data processing grows and memory capacity per server increases, we could see the use of data grids for high-speed analytics, possibly available as a cloud-based service.

on a proprietary hardware platform. Netezza also takes a hardware-software approach, leveraging the power of inexpensive parallel processing blades with a unique parallel relational database design. Greenplum and Aster Data, by contrast, take a software-only approach with their parallel relational platforms, relying on commodity hardware.

While parallel relational databases have their roots in data processing, there is now a clear focus on data analytics. For example, Greenplum is specifically targeting data analytics instead of online transaction processing, which has been the domain of traditional relational databases. Greenplum and Aster Data include a number of analytics tools, pre-built modules for commonly-used algorithms and tight integration with analytic products such as R. (Greenplum supports parallelized execution of R programs across Greenplum nodes). Greenplum also has Alpine Miner, a graphical tool for developing analytic algorithms from reusable components without having to write code. The algorithms are then executed on Greenplum nodes.[85] There is also the open source MADlib library of mathematical, statistical and machine learning algorithms optimized for parallelized execution.[86]

ONE SIZE NO LONGER FITS ALL

For decades the relational database has been the primary, if not only, way to handle enterprise data. Now there are many tools available to enterprises to address their data processing needs. One size no longer fits all. (See Figure 10.)

Enterprises will need to develop architecture roadmaps in which both relational and non-relational products can easily coexist in a single environment.[87] For example, Cloudera and Membase (now Couchbase) have combined an in-memory NoSQL database with Hadoop to produce online advertising and content targeting systems for AOL and ShareThis, where decisions must be made within 40-100 milliseconds of a person requesting a Web page.[88] Another example is Greenplum HD, which uses Hadoop's strength in processing unstructured data to transform and load data into Greenplum in a structured format, where Greenplum's analytics engine can take over. DataStax, the company that maintains the Apache Cassandra NoSQL database, has released its own Hadoop distribution called Brisk that allows organizations to access their data via either Hadoop or Cassandra without any transformation of the underlying data.[89]

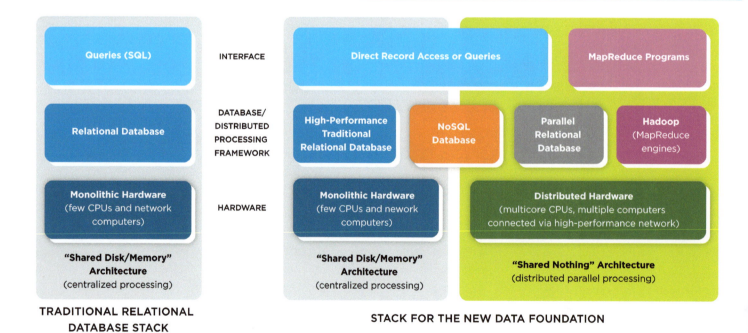

Figure 10 The traditional relational database stack, a staple of enterprise computing for decades, has evolved to a more varied data foundation.

Source: CSC

IBM also recognizes the power of combining non-relational and relational platforms with its BigInsights initiative, which leverages and extends Hadoop for enterprise deployments. BigInsights provides interoperability with DB2, Netezza, IBM Smart Analytics System data warehousing solutions and Oracle. IBM has introduced a tightly integrated solution where queries can be automatically distributed between DB2 and Hadoop as required. In addition to using open source software such as Pig, Hive, HBase, Avro, Lucene and Oozie, IBM will be adding new tools such as BigSheets, Jaql and SystemT advanced text analytics to help people manipulate big data in the Hadoop Distributed File System (HDFS). IBM Research has a number of advanced analytic capabilities in early testing with customers that will be forthcoming, and IBM's Watson used Hadoop knowledge and skills as part of its successful Jeopardy! performance.[90]

The importance of integrating different technologies is also reflected in market moves (recall Figure 1):

- EMC's acquisition of Greenplum and Teradata's acquisition of Aster Data bolster the competition and growth of these new database designs.[91]

- Netezza and Cloudera have established a relationship to integrate their platforms, strengthening the MapReduce functionality in Netezza's platform.[92]

- IBM's acquisition of Netezza puts more muscle behind MapReduce in the enterprise, IBM's position in the analytics market, and Netezza's approach (which uses IBM hardware).

- IBM's, Greenplum's (EMC), MapR's and Yahoo's focus on commercial Hadoop puts pressure on Cloudera.

The foundation of our data processing world is changing. We are shifting from shared disk/memory to shared nothing architectures, from centralized big-box processing to distributed commodity parallel processing, from separate analytics to in-database analytics. We are no longer restricted to our stove-piped relational database systems or warehouses; instead, we can use a variety of technologies including non-relational databases, MapReduce and federated mechanisms. And, we can archive forever.

There is a desire, if not a mandate, to break from the past and tap these new areas. Organizations are finding novel ways of working with data and are at the beginning of a new journey that is inspiring, innovative and happening right now. Organizations must resist clinging to the status quo and seize the opportunity to rebuild the data foundation to "connect the dots" and bring new competitiveness and performance to the enterprise.

THE NEW ALCHEMY:
CONNECTING THE DOTS

Today's new alchemy is about connecting the dots to turn discrete nuggets of information into gold. Thus continues the march of the Data rEvolution, from building the data foundation to driving new business opportunities.

For Netflix, it was so important to make good movie recommendations based on customer viewing data that the company sponsored a $1 million contest in 2009 for an algorithm that would improve recommendations by at least 10 percent.[93] For a hospital, it was so important to minimize unnecessary hospitalizations that it sponsored a $3 million contest for an algorithm that would analyze patient data to predict hospitalizations, so appropriate care plans could be implemented and hospitalizations averted.[94] For Amazon, it was so important to minimize costly returns that it created a set of algorithms, patented in December 2010, for letting recipients convert an undesired gift to a desired one *before* the gift is sent.[95]

This is data-driven business. Data-driven business demands a shift from collecting to connecting. Because data on its own is meaningless – the number 42 could represent the temperature outside, a test score, the price of dinner, the number of friends in your social network – data must be imbued with context to give it meaning, to make it unambiguous, to make it exciting. Thus our computers must capture not only the discrete data – numbers, text, images, sounds, videos and documents – but also the relationships that connect the data. Without these relationships we are left with a fragmented picture. Meaning and insights can only be derived as the various data sets are brought together relating the who, what, when, where, how and why of the story. (See Figure 11.)

This connectedness is fueling a new kind of discovery. People are using social networks to draw their own connections between friends, things, events, likes, dislikes, places,

ideas and emotions. Governments are analyzing social networks to thwart terrorist acts.[96] Businesses are mining

> ## This connectedness is fueling a new kind of discovery.

social and transactional information for connections that will help them discover new opportunities – and ultimately bring them closer to you, your friends, your behaviors and your tastes. Scientists are bridging the intellectual gap by building massive grids of connected data, gathering points

Figure 11 **DATA, DATA EVERYWHERE – WITH MANY STORIES TO TELL**

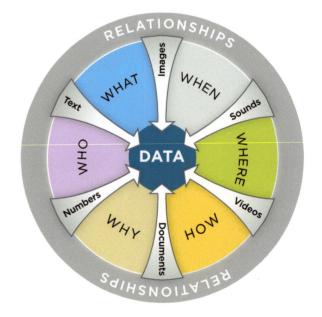

Source: CSC

of view in multidisciplinary global experiments. Academics are beginning to use analytics to study the humanities.[97]

All of this is generating a new breed of technologies and techniques for creating context and pulling together disconnected data to yield meaning. First we will explore some high-value examples of context. Then we will look at ways to forge deeper connections among disparate data.

CONTEXT COUNTS

Time, location and situational awareness are three important elements of context, addressing the who, what, when, where, how and why. They illustrate how essential context is for understanding data and making decisions.

Timing Is Everything. One way to predict future events, as well as examine past and present events, is to analyze data using time as a reference point. Recorded Future uses temporal analysis to relate people, places and events by time. The company's technology aggregates temporal information from the Web (e.g., articles, blogs, financial databases, comments) and behind the corporate firewall. It uses input from past trends and current activities to forecast behavior and issue "Futures," email alerts about predicted events.

Whereas a typical search does not understand "what will happen in Baghdad *next week*," Recorded Future does. People enter query terms in three simple search boxes for "What," "Who/Where" and "When." The system uses natural language processing and temporal reasoning to identify temporal signals in the data and match them to your query. Signals include phrases like: next week, last spring, this weekend, in June, in 2011, planning to meet on Thursday.

Recorded Future can perform a "pattern of life" analysis to identify all relevant activities pertaining to an individual's life, and show the results in a timeline using the company's Temporal Event Index. Whereas Twitter is about "right now," Recorded Future is about past, present and future.

Recorded Future factors in sentiment analysis (is what people are saying good or bad) and source credibility (e.g., a document from a government agency has greater weight than a blog post). So, for example, the technology can show positive and negative sentiment over time, as well as frequency and strength of mentions ("momentum"). Organizations can use Recorded Future for brand monitoring, competitive intelligence, equities research, research on a public figure or event, and other activities.[98] (See Figure 12.)

Location, Location, Location. Location has long been an important way to define context, and it is becoming increasingly critical.

Advances with location data are taking logistics in the enterprise to new levels. CSC's Logistics Center of Excellence (COE) calls it "enterprise visibility." Enterprise visibility integrates location, distance and status data with business information to create actionable intelligence. Improving enterprise visibility accelerates workflow, lowers costs and improves the speed and accuracy of delivery. The COE's signature tracking technology, OmniLocation®, is being used in a variety of ways including: connecting doctors to at-home patients for after-hours visits, monitoring the location and

Figure 12 Recorded Future shows search results for major solar investments in a timeline. The blue indicates momentum, or frequency of mentions, and the bubbles indicate number of sources (larger for more sources).

Source: Recorded Future

I NEED TO KNOW NOW

Often, *when* you get a result is as important as the result itself. The context at that moment in time helps shape the value of the results. Detecting and fixing problems on production lines as they happen, or correctly predicting trends in the stock market, could mean success for an organization over competitors.

Increasingly, we need results right now – in real time. Whereas in the past people queried data that was refreshed daily via batch processes, today many industries, such as telecommunications, finance and manufacturing, need the data to be updated immediately.

Such real-time analytics poses two challenges. First, there are now significantly more data inputs that need to be recorded (e.g., location data from smartphones and environmental sensors that provide more frequent readings). Second, some organizations are now using more sophisticated algorithms to take advantage of this extra data (e.g., stock market predictions for agricultural companies may take into account up-to-date weather forecasts). However, it is difficult to perform all necessary analytical calculations in real time, as the new data inputs keep coming in and complex algorithms require significant processing time.

Distributed processing frameworks like MapReduce can greatly speed up data processing for extremely large data sets, so batch processes can be run more frequently and deliver analysis results in near real time.

In situations where frequently executed batch processing is not sufficient, an event-driven architecture can be used. "Stream" processing is one example of this and is now well established, especially in financial services. Input data is processed as soon as it arrives, and not batched into large chunks. This essentially averages out the computing load over time. Processing may include filtering to remove outlier data points or aggregation to provide a more manageable data set for batch processors like MapReduce to take over. Researchers at CERN use this technique to manage the massive data volumes from their scientific experiments.[99]

Stream processors can also be used to detect complex events in incoming data and trigger appropriate actions, such as notifying traders when a combination of stock prices rises above a defined limit. Another example of a triggered action may be to start batch re-processing of a predictive model when discrepancies between model and actual values exceed a certain threshold; the model can then be kept up-to-date instead of waiting for the next scheduled batch run.

In terms of commercially available stream processing products, StreamBase is used in Bridgewater Associates' trading system, an investment company that manages $150 billion in funds.[100] IBM has released InfoSphere Streams, a product that can also handle unstructured data (e.g., audio, video, medical waveforms). InfoSphere Streams has been used by a number of telecommunications companies for real-time billing, including one in Asia that handles six billion call detail records a day (100,000 records per second at peak).[101] BackType Technology, a start-up company developing a real-time-capable social media analysis platform, will be open-sourcing its distributed and fault-tolerant stream processing engine called Storm.[102]

Recently, some work has been done by Yahoo and University of California, Berkeley to add stream processing capabilities to Hadoop. This would allow MapReduce to perform complex processing on streamed input data as it arrives, as well as provide access to approximate results as soon as calculations are completed.[103] This could be a "best of both worlds" all-in-one solution for complex real-time analytics.

physical condition of jet engines being delivered, guiding the workflow of field technicians (see Figure 13), managing marine traffic on the Chesapeake Bay, tracking cyclists along a 1,500 kilometer, 10-day charity event in Australia, and presenting directions and delivery information to consumers about postboxes in the United Kingdom (a smartphone app).

The future of enterprise visibility lies in faster and more comprehensive capabilities through technologies like wireless automatic identification and data capture (AIDC) – which includes RFID, bar codes, sensors, GPS, WiFi and biometrics – and real time locating systems (RTLS).

RTLS's are a form of RFID that can track the real time physical location, and often the condition, of assets and people in real time. Precyse Technologies has developed an innovative

employees wear a special tracking badge that signals where they are, whether inside or outside, and if they have fallen. The badge is also used to send and receive security alerts.

Better location data also means smarter marketing. Now that common devices such as smartphones can capture location-based information via GPS or other means, essentially every person with a smartphone has turned into a sensor. Organizations can use these new sensors as a source of valuable information about customers, which can then be used to provide advanced location-based services back to customers.

One way to leverage location data is through crowdsourcing. This is where citizens record and upload location-based data for others to use; this data is anonymized and essen-

Figure 13 CSC's OmniLocation tracking system is integrated with field service systems to track and coordinate field technicians. The system shows current location of the technician (yellow), the location of his assignments (blue dots), routing to the chosen assignment (blue line), navigation to that location (center pane), and details of the work order (lower left pane). CSC locations in the region are also shown (red).
Source: CSC

approach to RTLS, implementing a "last-mile" asset network to generate real-time asset information from location and condition sensors, which measure things like motion and temperature. Precyse and the CSC Logistics COE have created an RTLS that integrates active RFID with GPS, enabling two-way communication for alerts and control of sensors and infrastructure via smartphone or other Internet-connected device. CSC has integrated the Precyse iLocate RFID middleware with OmniLocation, which serves as the analysis, presentation and control interface. The result: smarter logistics and better personnel safety. CSC and Precyse are developing a solution to track employees in a harsh production environment;

tially becomes "open sourced." In the midst of recent furor around unauthorized logging of customer location data on iPhones and Android smartphones, crowdflow.net asked people to upload the offending location log files to its site in order to build a global map of cellular and WiFi networks.[104] Another example is SimpleGeo, which provides an API for developers to build location-based services in the cloud.[105] Part of its offering is a database of location "points of interest," to which people using the service can contribute.

There's more in store as location continues to answer the "where."

NETWORK ANALYTICS –
WHAT YOUR NETWORK DATA CAN TELL YOU

Hal Stern, Vice President and Chief Architect, Juniper Networks

The data riding on the network "knows," but teaching the network to make decisions on that data is where the future of network analytics lies.

Traditionally, applications demand resources from networks. Bandwidth, latency limits, secure tunnels between end points, and flexibility in provisioning new hardware onto the network are typical of application-centric views of the network. However, the network itself generates significant quantities of data that can lead to optimization and revenue enablers at the data center, service and application levels.

As networks carry more traffic of increasingly varied characteristics (from streaming video to multi-terabyte map-reduce operations to mobile access to enterprise applications), that traffic becomes more bursty and unpredictable in both time and space. Network analytics provides insight into the points of production, consumption and data flow between the networks. In other words, in addition to filling resource requests (utilitarian), the network can provide rich data to optimize the request fulfillment as well as prompt new, higher-level queries (smarts).

The need for network-generated "big data" is highlighted by what software pioneer Peter Deutsch termed the Fallacies of Distributed Applications more than 20 years ago. At that time, applications that spanned more than one machine were rare; today it's hard to find an application that embeds fewer than a handful of networks and data centers. Deutsch posited that developers would make bad assumptions about network latency (near zero), bandwidth (near infinite), transit cost (near zero), security and points of control.

Network analytics can address these assumptions, providing details on the actual network data flows, users, service subscribers and policy enforcement actions that paint a "weather map" of potential trouble spots. By collecting data from the "ground up" from the network, analysts can identify problems such as inefficient distribution of an application's components across the network, or contention for an intra-data center link that is affecting application performance as a large Hadoop job executes.

Mobility has made network analytics even more valuable due to the decoupling of producers and consumers of enterprise data from the network

fabric between them. The origin and destination for a large network data flow are rarely co-located and in many cases involve third parties. Thus it is much harder to understand data traffic and bottlenecks. Consider, for example, that 22 percent[106] of U.S. residential broadband traffic comes from Netflix streaming videos – an "over the top" (OTT) service that needs to be managed at both the ingress and egress points of an intermediate carrier's network.

If "where" remains a critical question to address congestion through resource optimization, better instrumentation and data from the network give us further insight into the mechanics of accessing OTT services and those hosted by service providers, and into the costs and issues associated with delivering them over a collection of networks. This is where good grounding in networked big data analytics can make a difference in network efficiency.

Situational Awareness. Situational awareness brings together many dimensions of context, from time and location to terrain, weather, objects and other elements. The essence of situational awareness is situational intelligence: a unified, consistent, up-to-date picture of all relevant information for a given situation. Situational intelligence correlates massive amounts of disparate data to facilitate immediate and informed decision-making. Using situational intelligence, people can easily recognize abnormal conditions and take prompt remedial action using defined rules and processes.

Space-Time Insight provides near real-time geospatial views and analytics for situational intelligence, a new breed of software that helps organizations make critical decisions faster to protect lives, property and profits. Situational intelligence correlates data from multiple sources to identify problem areas, determine root causes, and guide people to decisions using cues and alerts based on embedded business rules. (See Figure 14.)

Figure 15 SCORE-IO provides situational awareness for U.S. Navy training exercises.

Source: CSC

Figure 14 In this energy management example, the situational intelligence and awareness console federates geospatial intelligence, visualization, data and enterprise applications to alert operators and enable them to detect, analyze, and act on risk and revenue situations related to their smart grid in near real-time speed.

Source: Space-Time Insight

Space-Time Insight focuses on critical infrastructure such as utilities, energy, telecommunications and transportation. The company's software incorporates location, terrain, weather, time, node (e.g., sensor) and enterprise data

(e.g., ERP systems, security systems). The technology integrates, correlates and visualizes the data to deliver insights on evolving situations so that action can be taken. For example, in the utilities industry, if suppliers know a heat wave is imminent, they can ramp up production, notify customers to raise thermostats to avoid a brown-out, or raise thermostats themselves remotely. Being able to monitor demand in near real time and avoid a total grid shutdown that puts safety and property at risk makes more business sense than, literally, operating in the dark.

"With situational intelligence enterprises can analyze their resources across location and time, see the complete big picture of an evolving situation, and rapidly respond to, or even avoid, service disruptions," says Rob Schilling, CEO of Space-Time Insight.

Another example where situational awareness is critical is the battlefield. SCORE-IO, a 2011 CSC Chairman's Award for Excellence winner, provides 3D real-time situational awareness for U.S. Navy training exercises. The system tracks aircraft, ships and submarines, drawing on a variety of sensors at sea and in the air: surface and low-altitude radar, GPS, daytime and thermal cameras, identification "friend or foe" (IFF) systems and unmanned aerial vehicle (UAV) systems. All of this information is presented on a 3D virtual globe (NASA World Wind open source software), which may include up to 1,000 participants (trainees and trainers) during the exercise. (See Figure 15.)

Situational awareness is a key tenet of the U.S. Department of Homeland Security's Einstein cyber security program.

An important component of the solution is a distributed analytics system, which aggregates and analyzes data from network protection devices, and alerts Security Operations Centers to possible threats. This system is also used to share actionable intelligence between trusted US-CERT (United States Computer Emergency Readiness Team) partners so that attack signatures identified by one organization can be used to bolster security at other partners.[107]

FORGING DEEPER CONNECTIONS

People are always seeking to connect the data dots to form a more complete view of information. There are informal and formal ways to do this, depending on the situation. Informal ways employ a loose coupling between data and terms, while formal ways follow strict rules, structures and agreed-upon terms. We will explore the less formal approach of folksonomies first, followed by the more formal approaches of semantics and linked data.

Personalizing the Context: Folksonomies. The urge to connect the dots is readily apparent in the consumer realm, where data runs rampant (think social networks) and there is a crying need to organize it (in some fashion). Many people use tagging to bring some sense of order to all the photos, videos, blogs and newspaper articles they encounter.

Tagging is an example of a folksonomy, an informal, grass-roots classification system that enables individuals to define their own context and personalize data for their own use. This is in contrast to a taxonomy, which is a broad formal classification, such as the well-established taxonomy for classifying plants and animals. With folksonomies, people are not so much classifying as providing meaning based on their particular context. An article on health informatics might be tagged "healthcare" by one person and "analytics" by another.

Folksonomies are important because, as the name implies, they are informal, personal and flexible. They give people

> With folksonomies, people are not so much classifying as providing meaning based on their particular context.

greater ability to shape data to their needs and define relationships dynamically. The same data can be viewed from multiple perspectives (tags), all of which are valid.

These different "crowdsourced" perspectives on data can be used to support practical applications. For example, Freebase is a large, open source repository of information ranging from the sciences to government census information to sports. The dataset was built by, and is updated by, individuals using a folksonomy approach, not a formal ontology. As such, Freebase provides a way to grow the vocabulary people need to make the connections they want in Web data. Through Google's acquisition of Freebase's creator, Metaweb, Google aims to give people more relevant search results by leveraging the relationships and connections in the Freebase semantic knowledge base.[108]

Another folksonomy example, also from Google, is Image Labeler. Google created Image Labeler from the ESP Game, a project from Carnegie Mellon University, where people try to label images with the same tags as other randomly selected people. These common tags are then used to improve Google's image search application. Similar "games with a purpose" (GWAPs) have emerged to collect tags for music (Tag a Tune) and common sense knowledge (Verbosity).[109]

However, the flexibility of folksonomies can be a double-edged sword. While folksonomies make context more personal, the tags are harder for machines to interpret and understand, and hence more difficult to use in automated analysis tools. People can easily determine whether the tags "cloud" and "cloud_computing" refer to the same concept by analyzing the surrounding context, but this is vastly more difficult for a computer to do. However, formal techniques such as semantics and linked data allow us to forge deeper connections that can be understood unambiguously by people and machines alike.

Semantics. Semantics create connections based on meaning and offer a structured approach for linking data across data sets to make dynamic connections and tap data from unanticipated sources. These connections are forged by applying semantic technologies (e.g., the Resource Description Framework, or RDF, to describe relationships between items; Uniform Resource Identifiers (URIs), to identify the items; and OWL, a language for authoring ontologies).

There are two important movements driving semantics forward. First, industries are leveraging semantic technologies to enable better data integration between industry partners. By formally representing the alignment of meanings and vocabularies, organizations can create deeper data interoperability. One example of this is IBM's Reference Semantic Model (an extension of ISO 15926, the standard for process plant data). RSM is designed for manufacturing companies (process industries, oil and gas, automotive, aerospace) to drive data synergy among measurements, planning and scheduling, life cycle management and more.[110]

Second, on a broader scale, the Semantic Web movement is working to bring meaning to just about everything the World Wide Web touches. "The vision of the Semantic Web is a powerful global web of data with semantic context. It will usher in a new world of reasoning, linked data, text analytics, natural language processing, advanced search and machine learning," declares semantics expert Tony Shaw, founder of Dataversity.

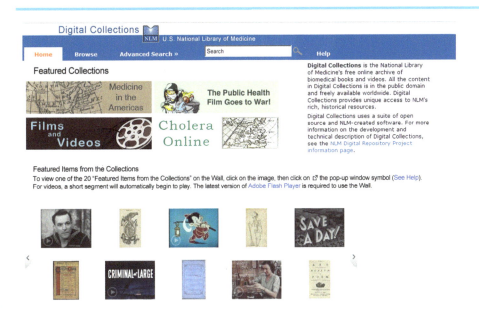

Figure 16   The U.S. National Library of Medicine Digital Collections site uses structured data relationships to help people find biomedical books and films.

Source: U.S. National Library of Medicine, http://collections.nlm.nih.gov/

> **The vision of the Semantic Web is a powerful global web of data with semantic context. It will usher in a new world of reasoning, linked data, text analytics, natural language processing, advanced search and machine learning.**

The U.S. National Library of Medicine's Digital Collections Web site has recently gone through the first phase of this transformation. NLM Digital Collections uses Semantic Web technologies (RDF) to describe relationships between items in the repository including books, images, films and collections. (See Figure 16.) The RDF metadata enables the repository software to easily navigate the relationships between items and present them to people.

NLM Digital Collections also uses RDF to represent descriptive metadata about items in the repository, like title of work, author and subject. The descriptive metadata is used to do field-based and author-based search for books and videos, such as "find works authored by John Snow."

The next step is semantic search. In the future, NLM envisions extending the metadata to enable searches such as "find works authored by anybody educated at the University of London." The repository software would search the metadata and find three cholera books written by John Snow, the father of epidemiology, who was educated at the University of London.

"RDF helps connect the dots by injecting the data with meaning and creating rich relationships among the data, making it easier to find what you're looking for," says Ed Luczak of CSC, lead architect for the NLM Digital Collections repository. "RDF is a semantic building block that paves the way for better search and discovery, which is especially important as the repository grows."

Semantics are a critical part of computer-based under-standing – of being able to present the right answer at the right moment in the right context. Without good semantics, data can be misinterpreted because the context is misunderstood or not understood at all. This was demonstrated vividly by IBM's Watson when, in a rare erroneous move, it guessed Toronto as an American city.[111] Its response missed the context, which was immediately apparent to a human but not apparent to the machine. Context is what will matter to achieve better machine discernment and predictions.

Linked Data. The Linked Data movement also leverages the semantic technologies just described, but does so with a little less definition. Instead of a specific vocabulary, linked data employs an agreed-upon format, an approach described by Web creator and Semantic Web visionary Tim Berners-Lee as "little pieces, loosely joined."[112] Linked data is a "bottom up" approach because anyone can add links – join their data to the linked data community – as long as their links conform to the linked data format.

Important public databases in government, life sciences (NLM and beyond) and media are now finding their way into the linked data movement. (See Figure 17.) Participants include Freebase, *The New York Times*, the U.S. government, the U.K. government, Linked Sensor Data (Kno.e.sis) and some 200 others. Very quickly your data becomes part of a broader community of connections by simply adhering to the linked data construct.

The U.S. government's initiative (Data.gov) is about "serendipitous data discovery," emphasizes Jeanne Holm, evangelist, Data.gov. Data.gov has 400,000 data sets for areas including health, law, energy, science and education. The initiative is building communities, such as Health.Data.gov, Law.Data.gov, and Energy.Data.gov, where people can discuss the data, point to other related data sources, share applications and visualizations, and issue challenges for new applications. "It's one thing to make data available, but we want to use these communities as platforms for innovation," Holm asserts.

For example, Health.Data.gov helped spawn a new company, Asthmapolis.com, which aids asthma sufferers. By giving people GPS-equipped inhalers, Asthmapolis.com records the time and location of inhaler use, aggregates this data, and provides a new source of data for physicians, scientists and public health officials to use to improve asthma management and identify asthma-related triggers in the environment. Patients can use the results to avoid an area, and city governments can use the results to change zoning laws, enforce regulations, or put pressure on a facility to reduce its asthma-triggering emissions (e.g., dust, pollutants). The idea is to understand how certain places can affect health and then take action to promote better health.

"We want to use data to help individuals and communities change behaviors and outcomes," Holm explains. "With Asthmapolis.com, the goal is improved health outcomes and lower healthcare costs overall by reducing asthma attacks."

LINKED DATA – AN EXPANDING COMMUNITY OF CONNECTIONS

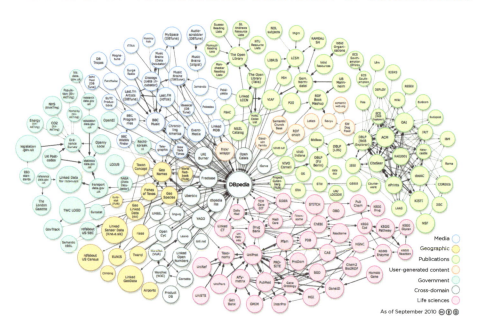

Media
Geographic
Publications
User-generated content
Government
Cross-domain
Life sciences

As of September 2010

Figure 17 There are over 200 data sets that are part of the Linked Open Data movement. Arrows indicate at least 50 links between two data sets.

Source: Linking Open Data cloud diagram by Richard Cyganiak and Anja Jentzsch, September 2010, http://lod-cloud.net/. This diagram is part of the Linking Open Data (LOD) W3C community project.

Other Data.gov innovations include linking data for finding the best hospitals near you to treat your specific illness (e.g., UCompareHealthCare.com); finding assisted living facilities in your area and their health ratings, morbidity ratings and specializations (Clinical Quality Linked Data[113]); and making EPA data on radiation levels on the West Coast (and nation-wide) publicly available in the aftermath of the Japanese tsunami and nuclear disasters in March 2011 (RadNet[114]).

As Data.gov works to link data sets across cities, states, tribes and federal agencies, it is also focused on global col-laboration. The WC3 has started a Government Linked Data Working Group and an eGovernment Interest Group to fos-ter global government linked data.[115] Holm chairs the lat-ter group and is working closely with Berners-Lee to help make his Semantic Web vision a reality.

The U.K. government (Data.gov.uk), a member of the work-ing group, is using linked data to share national data online. The site has over 6,200 data sets including data on health, transportation, government spending, tourism, crime and the environment. From researchers to consumers, people can access this data, connect it to their own data, and do their own analysis. One of the featured applications is OpenCorporates, an open database of corporations around the world with information on over eight million companies.

Elsewhere, the power of a vast network of linked data has been demonstrated in the Linked Clinical Trials project. LinkedCT aims to publish the first open Semantic Web data source for medical clinical trials data.[116] The data exposed by LinkedCT is generated by transforming existing data sources of clinical trials into RDF, and discovering links between the records in the trials data and several other data sources.[117] These external data sources are extensive, including DBpedia and YAGO (linked data sources, based on Wikipedia articles, about diseases and drugs), DailyMed (information about marketed drugs published by the NLM)

and Diseasome (information about disorders and disease genes).[118] The project links clinical trials and outcomes to yield new research opportunities.

"All these movements are part of a broader trend to unlock siloed data, just as the Web unlocked siloed documents," observes Paul Gustafson, director of CSC's Leading Edge Forum. "Governments, research institu-tions and, eventually, corporations are striving to unlock their data so more minds can work a problem, reveal new insights, or create an innovative app."

> All these movements are part of a broader trend to unlock siloed data, just as the Web unlocked siloed documents.

From national intelligence to healthcare to commerce, organizations need guidance on how to connect the dots. In an instructive blog post, Tom Davenport, professor of management and information technology at Babson College and co-author of *Analytics at Work: Smarter Decisions, Better Results*, identifies eight steps for how to connect disparate pieces of information about the same person, organization or entity.[119] He cautions that connecting the dots is valuable but difficult. It starts with having clean data and ends with having an action plan for when the key pattern or event is identified.

Connecting the dots is one thing, but putting them to use is quite another. The data leads the way to insights, but it is up to us to take action. This is one of the challenges of the Data rEvolution.

ENABLING THE PREDICTIVE ENTERPRISE: STRATEGIES TO UNDERSTAND, ANTICIPATE AND PLAN

The data continuum starts with raw dots and builds to the ultimate goal: rich insights. Increasingly, organizations have better information and tools for looking ahead and are using these capabilities to understand, anticipate and plan. The result is the predictive enterprise, which can be explored through the lens of several enabling techniques. These range from the ability to ask better questions and plumb the depths of social data to more widespread use of predictive analytics, advanced models and analytics for everyone.

FOLLOWING CLUES AND CUES

In the enterprise, where disparate data runs rampant, vendors are working to integrate data so that better questions can be asked. "Search has become dominant because it has been relatively painless, but with the proliferation of high-powered data and analytics tools, the new game will be about asking the right questions," declares Alex Black, senior partner, Enterprise Intelligence Practice, Strategic Services Group, CSC.

Endeca's MDEX engine addresses the ability to ask better questions, combining search engine plus analytic database

> Search has become dominant because it has been relatively painless, but with the proliferation of high-powered data and analytics tools, the new game will be about asking the right questions.

technologies and drawing on structured and unstructured data. Business people can do sophisticated searches on the fly and answer not only "What happened?" but "What do I do now?" Endeca's technology embraces semantics, but Endeca believes that ultimately people determine meaning. Endeca provides as many clues as possible to guide people to asking more refined questions so they can arrive at even better outcomes.

For example, a manufacturer with warranty claims coming in would routinely ask: How much have claims gone up for our top-selling product? There is a structured report for this, which answers: 45 percent. But now the manufacturer has additional questions: Is this normal? What is the answer by product version? By color? By model? Also: Why? Did we change suppliers? Parts? Processes? And: What are customers saying? Have their comments changed? How?

These discovery questions often end up in a business intelligence (BI) backlog. To address this, Endeca enables self-service discovery by business people. Using a point-and-click interface with a search box, people can do sophisticated searches and keep adjusting their queries to home in on exactly what they are looking for. Whether the engine is drawing information from a structured ERP system or from an unstructured wiki is transparent to the person, who simply sees the integrated results.[120]

Endeca has received accolades for its solution at Toyota, which lets quality engineers sift through six years of product and quality data from numerous systems in ways that were not previously possible, identifying patterns they would not have known to look for in the past.[121] For example, key questions Toyota needed to ask as a result of its gas pedal recall were:

- Which pedal assemblies are used in exactly which vehicles?
- What information do we have about the quality checks done for these pedal assemblies?
- Which assembly plants were used?
- Which warranty claims are valid?

Using Endeca's solution, Toyota could combine different data sets that were never intended to be combined, to get answers to these and other questions quickly. The solution analyzed more than 50 million records across 75 dimensions, enabling engineers to quickly navigate from alerts to individual transactions correlated across input systems, and saving engineers an estimated 800,000 hours annually in query processing time.[122]

These were queries Toyota didn't know it needed to ask until the reports of unintended acceleration started to occur. This was significant because traditionally data is modeled based on questions identified up front, and then conforming data goes into the model. Facing entirely new questions "after the fact," Toyota needed to leverage Endeca's fundamental technical innovation, which is that its engine does not use a pre-determined model for the data. Instead, all the data goes into the engine, and then a model (schema) emerges from the attribute pairs in the data, whatever they may be.

The data is broken into attribute pairs and indexed based on all the relationships between the attribute pairs. This highly granular approach is called a faceted data model because it lets people look at the data from multiple perspectives (facets) rather than through a rigid taxonomy, allowing repeated filtering to refine questions on the fly.

Endeca brings together data that was never designed to be combined, resulting in what the company calls "jagged data." The data does not line up neatly, and there are numerous diverse attributes. Jagged data, the new reality, needs to be harnessed for insights and decision-making. (See Figure 18.)

"Today's world is about volume, variety and volatility of both data *and decisions*," stresses Paul Sonderegger, chief strategist at Endeca. "It is now possible to inform a much greater diversity of decisions through data. The challenge is that the organization does not know what decisions will matter next week. That is why our focus is the data, not the structure, and showing every possible relationship in the data. This is a completely new approach that captures insights that could not be captured using the traditional BI approach."

A NEW WAY TO MODEL JAGGED DATA

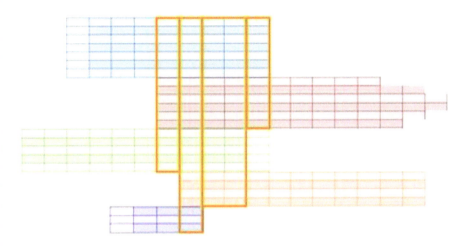

Figure 18 In today's data-diverse world, carefully modeled data from traditional business systems is combined with data from documents, notes, Web feeds and other databases, resulting in jagged data. Endeca's MDEX engine exploits jagged data, enabling it to be viewed from multiple perspectives so that people can ask better questions, see new patterns, and make informed decisions.

Source: Endeca

SOCIAL DISCOVERY

Social discovery has come to the fore in the last year with Facebook exceeding 750 million members and founder Mark Zuckerberg being named Person of the Year 2010 by *Time* magazine.[123] More and more, we are tapping social networks to problem-solve and derive deeper insights into customer attitudes. Such "social discovery" is rich with business implications as enterprises learn to leverage relationships and what people are saying online about products and services.[124]

Understanding relationships and what people say is what intelligence analysts have been doing for decades. But the meaning of relationships was tragically missed in the case of the 9/11 terrorist attacks, where it was later shown that all 19 hijackers had first- or second-degree relationships with the two original terrorist suspects.[125] A simple visualization later showed the connections. (Visualization goes hand-in-hand with relationship analysis and complex data and is discussed in the next chapter.)

The 9/11 example reinforces that connecting the dots is hard, and it is powerful. Companies want to figure out how to understand social patterns and what people are saying, good or bad – i.e., sentiment analysis. (See Figure 19.) Facebook, Twitter and others recognize the opportunity, creating APIs so enterprises can tap into the social mother lode.

Companies like Procter & Gamble (P&G), for whom brand image is extremely important, are proactively conducting sentiment analysis, mining comments, compliments and complaints. P&G, which has created a text analytics group, uses the same tools as intelligence agencies to "listen to"

online conversations and manage the P&G brand. It is another way of examining customer satisfaction, and, in a parallel with the intelligence world, it includes looking for nefarious activities, such as someone trouncing the brand.

Such a situation came to light regarding Pampers diapers when a small but irate group on Facebook claimed that a new version caused diaper rash. As word spread, both the stock price and sales fell. Although the issue was eventually settled in court, at the time P&G received kudos for its swift response, which included round-the-clock social media monitoring.[126]

Companies can use sentiment analysis to help them understand why customers buy. Exalead's CloudView 360 solution uses semantics and text analytics to find meaning across disparate data sets ranging from social data to structured ERP data.[127] The idea is to match the "why" inherent in social data with the "results" inherent in well-understood traditional data like ERP and CRM systems, sales spreadsheets and financial reports.

Figure 19 SENTIMENT ANALYSIS: PLUMBING THE DEPTHS OF COMMENTS, RATINGS AND OTHER SOCIAL DATA

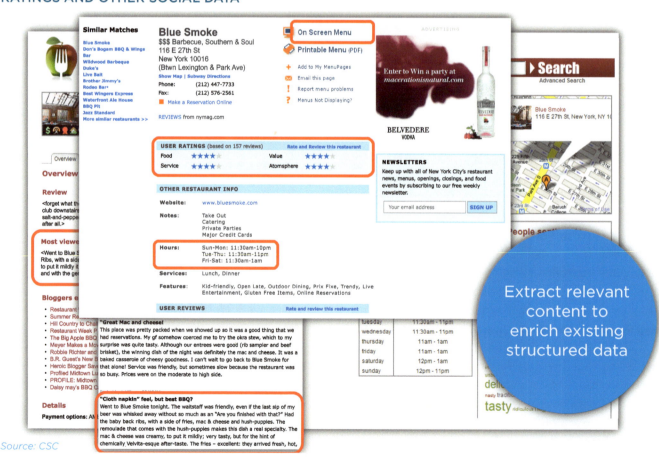

Source: CSC

Even financial traders are tapping sentiment analysis, using software to parse news reports, blogs and Twitter posts in an effort to keep a pulse on changing market moods. This auto-analysis of the news includes future innovations like monitoring and digesting broadcast TV and public statements by business executives.[128]

Other sentiment analysis vendors include Appinions and Lithium. Appinions culls data from blogs, Twitter, Facebook, news articles and elsewhere so organizations can understand who the key influencers are for a product or brand and build relationships with them ("influencer relationship management").[129] Lithium provides social media monitoring and e-commerce support to help organizations find, listen to and engage the "new social customer."[130]

ON THE PREDICTIVE EDGE OF ANALYTICS

As Recorded Future showed in the previous chapter, organizations need to answer questions about yesterday, make decisions about today, and perhaps most importantly, know how to plan for tomorrow. A world of data-backed predictions is opening up, driven by a combination of better and more data plus the desire to make predictions with increasing accuracy and speed. Examples of this new world are ordinary search data being repurposed to make predictions, predictive analytics being applied in near real-time to online activities, supply chain management becoming more predictive, and predictive analytics being used in everyday Web searches.

Search Patterns Predict. When simple search query data from Google turned out to be an accurate predictor of flu in the United States in 2008, a new method of predicting was born. Google's search data provided near real-time information – representing just a one-day lag, with data refreshed daily. Data from the U.S. Centers for Disease Control and Prevention had a one- to two-week lag and was updated weekly. Although the Google query data was not official medical data, it was good enough to give a rough indication of where flu was about to strike (confirmed by health agencies roughly two weeks later). Having more timely data enables earlier detection, essential for combating and lessening the impact of disease.[131]

The flu trend data was first published in 2009 in the journal *Nature*.[132] The technique, originally applied to the United States, has since been applied to 28 countries.[133]

The technique relies on a large amount of aggregated search data, so it works for areas with large populations using the Web. The technique also relies on historic public health data (surveillance reports) to determine the

> Using search data for predictions is an extraordinary repurposing of social data to predict real issues of public health, not to mention political events and other movements. Focus shifts from what people are saying (sentiment analysis) to what people are asking (query analysis).

effectiveness of the estimates. Google wants to apply the technique to more places and, if possible, to more diseases.[134] This is an extraordinary repurposing of social data to predict real issues of public health, not to mention political events and other movements. Focus shifts from what people are saying (sentiment analysis) to what people are asking (query analysis).

Another example of predictions based on search queries is the Web Bot Project, originally designed in the late 1990s to predict stock market trends by tracking keyword search terms. Based on proprietary software and algorithms that digest language patterns, Web Bot has since been used for predicting catastrophic events. Property and casualty insurers are on the leading edge of the insurance industry for using predictive analytics to hedge catastrophic risks, so they would seem a natural for using Web Bot predictions. However, Web Bot's perceived track record and the secretive nature of the underlying algorithms, which prevent scientific or actuarial scrutiny, keep the insurance industry from giving these predictions any real weight. Web Bot's full potential could lie ahead in conjunction with the explosion of social media and sentiment expression available for consumption and analysis. Whatever its future, the roots of Web Bot illustrate one of the most fascinating aspects of the Data rEvolution: using data in wholly new ways.

Predictions About You. Whereas Google's flu trends make predictions about large populations, other companies are making predictions about individuals. Online targeting platform company [x+1] provides a predictive optimization engine that can integrate with Nielsen consumer data to make "best guesses" about consumers on the Web. Capital One uses it to decide within a mouse click what credit card products to offer to first-time visitors of its site. Unlike Amazon, which uses in-house data about existing customers, Capital One uses third-party data plus data from the person's computer to create a profile of that person, whom it otherwise knows nothing about. For example, a person might be identified as a student in the Midwest and thus shown low-limit credit cards (many attributes are identified from thousands of pieces of data analyzed). It's all done in seconds, with results that many would consider good enough versus making no predictions at all.[135]

In another example of making predictions about individuals online, iovation predicts the "goodness" of an Internet-connected device using device recognition technology, sophisticated pattern matching, and device-based risk scoring. iovation can determine in nanoseconds whether the laptop, smartphone or tablet a person is accessing a Web site from is "safe" or tied to fraudulent activity, in which case the transaction can be blocked before it starts. iovation's device reputation service, used by online merchants to stop fraud, essentially "fingerprints" a device and then re-identifies it every time it accesses a Web site or application. The service is based on the company's knowledge base of 700 million devices and combines data about fraud and abuse from numerous global brands, customized business rules, device-account relationships, device profiles, "Real IP" (not proxy) connection and geolocation details, and transaction anomaly checks.[136] The technology's ability to aggregate trends, connect the dots and make predictions about devices anonymously and immediately is an important advance in fraud prevention because it does not rely on data supplied from a person, like name or address, which can be fraudulent. One can imagine applying iovation's extensive knowledge base to marketing and other activities as well. Indeed, BlueCava positions its device fingerprinting technology as a way to improve online advertising targeting (as well as identify fraud-tainted devices).

Predicting the Supply Chain. Demand management is becoming more precise as consumer product marketers improve their ability to predict, and shape demand for,

their products. Integrating data from multiple disparate sources, both internal and external, is the key. External data comes in the form of point-of-sale (POS) and inventory data from multiple retailers and syndicated data from data service companies such as IRI and Nielsen. Vision Chain is one company providing this integration, via its Keystone Demand Signal Repository, which collects data from multiple retailers and delivers it to the supplier, in near real time. Vision Chain's demand-driven analytics enable companies to answer questions like: How are my products selling? How did consumers respond to my promotion? How many days or weeks of supply are in stores? What stores have aged inventory? What were my core out-of-stock items yesterday and last week, and what are the potential ones currently? Vision Chain is developing predictive applications in areas such as promotion compliance: Does the store have the right levels of inventory at the right price for an upcoming promotion?

Related to supply chain management is energy management – monitoring energy consumption instead of product consumption. One company, GridGlo, combines real-time energy data from smart meters with historical and other data like weather and demographics to help utility companies predict demand.[137]

Instant Search. Google's use of predictive techniques to boost its flagship search underscores the power of predicting in a data-driven world. The Google Instant enhanced search service starts presenting search results as soon as a person starts typing a search term, using predictive analytics to guess the search term in advance and altering the results presented as the person types (i.e., narrows the search). Google claims that by presenting results up front and dynamically like this, people can complete their searches more quickly as well as do more refined searches on the fly.[138]

MIGHTY MODELS

Our predictive future will be driven by innovations involving rich semantics and large data sets, coupled with advanced data models. These models, like formulas for new drug compounds, are the magic behind gleaning insights from data.

We are creating new data models to support large volumes of data from new sources. The models allow people to comprehend the data and provide a standard way to define and organize the data so everyone is "on the same page."

These data models feed the expert models that make sense of the data and yield insights and results. Much the way people learn from experience, so too computers "learn" through expert models. Having more data is like having more experience – you get more learning, better expert models and better results.

More industries are starting to use expert models now that there is so much data available. In the past, there was not enough data available to make the model meaningful. Now there is.

At the same time, industries that have used advanced models for years now have more data to work with and more potential insights to glean. For example, CSC is developing an expert model for the insurance industry that simulates lifetime customer profitability. Although this is a common measure in other industries, there was no lifetime profitability simulation formula that could be leveraged across insurer product lines. For one thing, the data was not readily available for such a model. CSC addressed that with its insurance industry data model, which lets insurers see their fragmented data as a whole and drive insights from a customer perspective.

> **Having more data is like having more experience – you get more learning, better expert models and better results.**

The data model provisions the data for the expert model. The expert model simulates real-life customer behavior, which is then analyzed for making predictions about how to service, sell to, and build deeper relationships with existing customers, and attract new customers who match key characteristics of the best existing customers. Insurance has become an extremely competitive market in recent years, so having such data-driven insights can be crucial to success.

Across all markets, organizations are striving to make better predictions. Stock traders have been using predictive models to beat other traders for quite some time. With all the new data available, we can now build these models for other areas. Consider Google's natural language corpus (collection of text). Probabilistic models have been built from the corpus, a trillion-word data set developed from Web pages and published texts, to tackle a variety of problems: word segmentation, secret codes, spelling corrections, spam detection, author identification, document unshredding (reassembly), DNA sequencing, language translation and even the evolution of human culture ("culturomics").[139]

Big data reduction techniques like those used to create the Google corpus will likely result in many new reduced data sets, from which powerful probabilistic models will be built to address a variety of tasks. In fact, it is likely that a new breed of data processing techniques will emerge that are less dependent on deterministic models of information and more dependent on probabilistic models. (IBM's Watson used a probabilistic design.) As people gain a deeper understanding of probabilities shaped by massive data sets, this will reshape approaches for putting predictive powers to work, leading to more and better predictive analytics for better outcomes.

ANALYTICS FOR EVERYONE

As people demand more insights from the growing mass of data, they are getting the tools to analyze the data themselves – that is, to build and manipulate more sophisticated models. People are witnessing the democratization of data analytics.

For example, Revolution Analytics is commercializing R, the leading open source predictive analytics language, and bringing it to the masses, much like Red Hat and others have commercialized Linux. R has been around since 1993, with an open source community numbering millions worldwide. The language has historically been confined to a sophisticated community (statisticians and skilled programmers); Revolution Analytics plans to change that so that more people can build more advanced models.

By delivering an enhanced version of R for the enterprise, called Revolution R Enterprise, and including support, the company brings analytics to those who never had such tools before, and gives more powerful analytics to those who already have analytical tools. As it makes analytics more accessible, easier to use and more affordable, the company is setting up a disruptive innovation.[140]

CHALLENGES TO CONNECTING THE DOTS AND MAKING PREDICTIONS

"It's tough to make predictions, especially about the future."[141]
– Yogi Berra

The harder it is to connect the dots, the harder it is to make predictions. Indeed, when it comes to building systems for data-based decision-making, there are many challenges that illustrate the realities of integrating large databases that were not designed to be integrated. These challenges, outlined in a paper describing systems that integrate large public data sets for policy reform, include legal, ethical, technical and economic issues such as:[142]

- *Legal* – Can the data be shared and used for research and analysis "as is," in modified form (e.g., de-identified), or not at all?

- *Ethical* – Can or will the data be re-identified? Could the data be misused? Have confidentiality risks been minimized?

- *Technical* – Is data acquisition secure? Is the data accurate and complete? What are the rules for linking records?

- *Economic* – Who funds development and ongoing support for the integrated system, especially if its initial purpose has changed?

In addition to these issues, which apply to both the public and private sector, there is the human element.

Systems for decision-making are only as good as their users' training and foresight. Too often, those who could benefit the most are the least prepared to reap the benefits; no one wants to spend the time and money educating them. So these people either do not use the tools or glean only the most superficial insights commensurate with their level of expertise. On the flip side, those skilled at working with the data are typically not the people asking the really good business and policy questions.

Then there is the issue of data overload – of not being able to absorb and ferret out important patterns from all the data in a timely manner. In military situations with live combat and live data feeds, this can be fatal.[143]

Further, the age-old problem of not having useful keys to link information across systems, hampering people from understanding the full context of a given "dot," often leads to poor or mistaken interpretations.

Once the data dots are connected, however, it's important to be able to balance hard data and human intelligence.[144]

"In a best practices environment, data and statistical algorithms are deployed such that human knowledge can be naturally integrated; it's not an either-or situation," says Charles Troyer, consumer and retail practice director at CSC. "For example, consider a method that allows the input of the timing and parameters of a future retail promotion. The algorithms generate the most likely outcome of that event, and then allow the human to review, modify and finalize the prediction."

People can and should be tapped to help explain past and future performance. Better predictions will improve agility, risk management and performance in the enterprise.

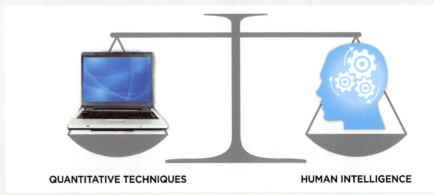

QUANTITATIVE TECHNIQUES   HUMAN INTELLIGENCE

Because Revolution Analytics's technology is rooted in open source, there is an abundance of R extensions (packages) – over 3,000 – from the open source community that

> **As people demand more insights from the growing mass of data, they are getting the tools to analyze the data themselves.**

can be adapted and applied. Revolution Analytics is focusing on bringing packages with commercial application to companies that need those advanced functions. For example, banks can use the portfolio optimization techniques in the Rmetrics suite of packages. Revolution Analytics is also bringing big data support to packages, such as enabling visualization of data sets with many millions of rows.

Two prominent markets for R are financial services and life sciences. Bank of America uses Revolution R to analyze and visualize gigabytes of multidimensional data for capital adequacy modeling, decision systems design and predictive analytics. Capital adequacy modeling is the process banks use to ensure they have sufficient cash in reserve in comparison to their outstanding loans. Revolution R speeds up analytic processes and enables rapid prototyping of models. Its visualization capabilities enable analysts to view complex, high-dimensional data sets more intuitively and make decisions about the most appropriate quantitative techniques that would be difficult if not impossible to do otherwise.[145]

CardioDX used Revolution R to analyze genomic data to create the first gender-specific diagnostic tests for heart disease. Revolution R was used to develop the diagnostic algorithm, which required extensive analysis of 10 gigabytes of data to identify what turned out to be 23 optimal genes for predicting heart disease. Blood samples from 42,000 patients were analyzed; each sample contained approximately 50,000 genes and 1-2 million pieces of genetic information. Revolution R was used for its speed, ease of parallelization, and ability to handle large data sets.

"There were millions of possible predictors. We got it down to 23 genes, with a few variations for males versus females," explains Mike Elashoff, director of biostatistics at CardioDx.

"Having fast statistical processing enables us to leverage genomic data for new diagnostic products and move healthcare a step closer to personalized medicine."

One of the major innovations that Revolution Analytics has brought to R is support for large data sets. Standard R requires all data to be loaded into memory on the workstation before it can be analyzed. Revolution R Enterprise includes extensions to optimize data file formats and memory access so that this restriction no longer applies. It can also parallelize processing across multiple CPU cores and multiple networked machines, leveraging shared nothing architecture to deliver high performance analytics. By using open source modules for connecting to data sources like Hadoop, NoSQL, relational databases and data warehouses, Revolution R enables people to use R to analyze large volumes of data in the enterprise, wherever it is stored.[146]

Revolution Analytics' effort to democratize analytics includes the RevoDeployR Web services framework, which lets developers incorporate R algorithms (created by others) without having particular knowledge of R itself. So, a sales person might see forecasts for product sales for the next three months (plus best-case and worst-case limits based on a 95 percent confidence interval) in a spreadsheet-based application or a BI dashboard, without ever knowing there is advanced predictive analytics going on behind the scenes. The sales person can benefit from the analytics, and the developer does not need to be a PhD statistician to deliver those benefits. More developers can deliver more analytic power to more people. (See Figure 20.)

In addition to sales data, an organization might use Revolution R for real-time analysis of operational data, such as analyzing equipment as it comes off the assembly line to look for failures so they can be handled right away. "If you are not analyzing this data, you're not competitive," asserts Jeff Erhardt, chief operating officer of Revolution Analytics. "Data is going to waste today. Organizations need to be able to analyze their data more easily and make decisions from it."

Also pursuing the democratization of data analytics is Fuzzy Logix. The company's in-database computation engine, DB Lytix, works with existing databases to make analytics easier to integrate into daily operations and more accessible to business people.

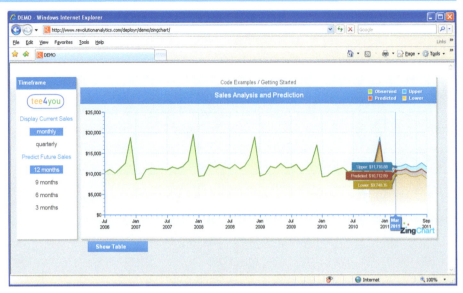

Figure 20 In this sales forecast application for a fictitious t-shirt company, a sales manager clicks at the left to select either quarterly or monthly data to predict sales for 3, 6, 9 or 12 months into the future. In the chart, predictions are shown in blue, red and tan for upper, predicted and lower values respectively; actuals are shown in green.

The application invokes two R scripts, one for aggregating the sales data and one for generating the plots. The application developer incorporates the scripts without having specific knowledge of R by using the RevoDeployR framework, which puts sophisticated analytics into the hands of application developers and, by extension, business people.

Source: Revolution Analytics

In-database analytics is about speed and efficiency. With in-database analytics, data doesn't have to be moved to an analytics server – which can account for up to 70-80 percent of processing time – but can be processed where it resides, saving time and enabling processing of larger data sets. (See Figure 21.)

> **Data is going to waste today. Organizations need to be able to analyze their data more easily and make decisions from it.**

"The analytics process can run 10 to 100 times faster by leveraging the existing database platform and moving the analytics to the database," says Mike Upchurch, Fuzzy Logix COO.

DB Lytix functions (algorithms) are embedded in the database or data warehouse and executed via simple SQL statements. Because SQL is widely used, this enables analytics to be integrated with standard processes, reports and applications that already use SQL queries. In addition, functions can be embedded into spreadsheets, Web pages and mobile apps. Thus, analysts who use SQL and even those with less SQL familiarity can invoke analytics – a much larger group than the highly specialized math and statistics PhDs who have traditionally been needed to do analytics.

"Our goal is to make analytics pervasive," Upchurch emphasizes. "To be most effective, analytics should be put in the hands of decision makers." For example, Fuzzy Logix embedded its analytics in Trident Marketing's business processes, notably telemarketing and online advertising, to improve the effectiveness of Trident's marketing campaigns significantly. (See the Great Expectations chapter.)

While enabling the pervasive deployment of analytics, in-database analytics also speeds development time for model builders. Organizations have reported up to a 10-fold increase in model-building efficiency due to gains in processing speed and the ability to work on all data without moving it.

Fuzzy Logix provides hardware, software and a library of over 800 quantitative functions so solutions can be built quickly. The company's technology works with a number of database platforms including those from Sybase/SAP, Netezza/IBM, Microsoft, Aster Data/Teradata, and Informix/IBM.

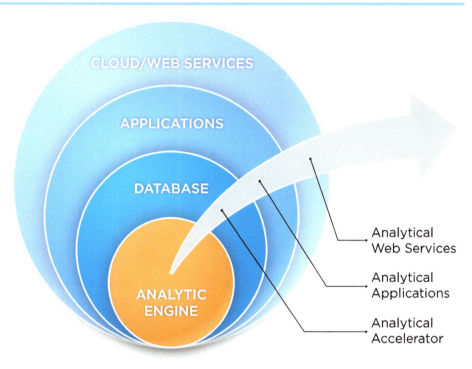

Analytical
Web Services

Analytical
Applications

Analytical
Accelerator

Figure 21 Fuzzy Logix enables pervasive analytics through "in-database" and in-GPU analytics, which can be embedded in enterprise applications and Web services and accessed by a broad user base.

Source: Fuzzy Logix

so they can analyze it themselves to stay on top of their health. The company is combining data analytics and mobile devices to help "tighten the feedback loop" between people and their chronic condition.[152] With data available via smartphone, patients can understand immediately how their condition has changed. Having timely feedback should help reinforce positive behaviors and improve health outcomes. The company will also analyze patient data for trends and share that with members.

The move to pervasive analytics reflects the natural progression from Software as a Service to Data as a Service to, now, Analytics as a Service. These are all distinct components of a business analytics solution that supports both scalability and mobility. Opera Solutions and Microsoft's Project Daytona are examples of the new Analytics as a Service.

Other moves making analytics pervasive include the rise of business intelligence apps for smartphones and tablets, such as apps from MicroStrategy Mobile, Roambi and MeLLmo;[147] browser-based tools like IBM BigSheets;[148] and easier-to-use analytics software such as Datameer Analytics Solution, the first Hadoop-based solution for big data analytics.[149] Google's preview release of its internal analytics software in the form of BigQuery, now part of Google Apps Script and Google Spreadsheets, and its release of Prediction API, which lets developers access Google's internal prediction algorithms, continue the democratization of the tools.[150] BigQuery can query 60 billion records in roughly five seconds, all in the cloud.[151] These tools unlock analytics from their specialized origins, shifting analytics to more people, closer to the business, so they can see first-hand how their business is performing and discover where new opportunities lie.

Consumers can get in on the analytics act too. Massive Health, a start-up focusing on healthcare, plans to create mobile applications that deliver data directly to patients

As organizations become more analytic, they are becoming more predictive. Many organizations collect enormous amounts of data, so they have the raw material. Even though they may not leverage it all or data may not be their core business, eventually enterprises will realize the full value inherent in their data and maximize its potential. This is just the beginning as tools improve and become more

The move to pervasive analytics reflects the natural progression from Software as a Service to Data as a Service to, now, Analytics as a Service.

widely available, and as an analytical culture takes hold that recognizes the power of the predictive enterprise.

SEEING IS BELIEVING:
VISUALIZATION AND VISUAL ANALYTICS

We are literally "wired" to see. Long before physicists postulated the existence of the photon, nature had evolved an apparatus (the retina and visual brain) that could transform a continuous stream of photons into a stream of neural impulses that represent the world we see. Remarkably, these impulses, or bits, that flow to your brain along roughly a million parallel fibers from each of your eyes transmit in aggregate roughly 20 million bits of visual information per second. What flows to your brain is not light, but rather an ingenious pattern of impulses that somehow gives rise to our ability to "see," to identify things, to make connections, to draw inferences, to pick out patterns and to form lasting visual memories.

The information world works in a similar way, transforming core data (photons, if you will) into higher and higher levels of abstraction that create representations and patterns people can work with ("see").

Today, as enterprises face mountains of information, new ways are emerging to visually represent information using a multitude of dimensions across time and space – a new form of 21st century digital cubism. The future of visualization must support analytical reasoning by representing information in any number of points of view, giving us the ability to draw correlations and make connections in an n-dimensional context. Speed, interaction and flexibility are essential, for context can change quickly, revealing a change in the story, and our interest in one point of view over another can shift in an instant.

We are challenged to graphically identify some "truth" from the dizzying arrays of information we are collecting and connecting, and then use visual imagery to accurately communicate our findings without bias, *letting the data tell the story*. We want to detect patterns. We want to spot outliers. We want to convey useful, actionable insights from billions of pieces of data. We want the ability to interact with the information so that we can each combine our intellect, insights, intuition and imagination into crafting a story that makes sense to us and that we can communicate to others.

These information challenges go beyond the realm of scientific graphics and have given rise to new visualization tools and techniques designed for data exploration and discovery. These tools, including relationship graphs and other new forms of imagery, are helping us manipulate, see and understand information in new ways.

VISUAL ANALYTICS: PUTTING THE HUMAN IN THE LOOP

If "seeing is believing," then how much better if we could be part of the picture. What if we could depart from

> We are challenged to graphically identify some "truth" from the dizzying arrays of information we are collecting and connecting, and then use visual imagery to accurately communicate our findings without bias, *letting the data tell the story.*

being passive observers of information and images to becoming interactive participants who can view, filter, rearrange and align connections to help make sense of the information for ourselves?

The future is to empower people to discover and tell their own story with tools that let them explore and manipulate data to reveal the story that is of importance to them. Identifying relationships among would-be terrorists and unearthing fraud rings are examples.

"The essence of information visualization is to accelerate human thinking with tools that amplify human intelligence," observes Ben Shneiderman, a pioneer in the human-computer interface at the University of Maryland.

Enter a new era in information visualization called *visual analytics*: analytical reasoning supported by highly interactive visual interfaces. People are using visual tools and techniques to manipulate data to derive insights from massive, dynamic and often conflicting data; to detect the expected and discover the unexpected; to provide timely, defensible and understandable assessments; and to communicate assessments effectively for action. (See Figure 22.)

"Overview first, zoom and filter, then details-on-demand." This mantra is drilled into the heads of Shneiderman's graduate students. Give people control so they can help themselves manage the flood of data to do their own discovery and tell their own story. Whether one is looking for relationships, clusters, outliers, gaps or other types of patterns in million- and billion-record data sets, it is important to hand capabilities over to people and enable them to create connections and apply the human touch to refine and resolve entities and relationships.

To the visual analytics practitioner, entities are not another name for the tables found in relational databases. Entities are any person, place, thing or event that may be related. Powerful next-generation visual analytics tools like those from Visual Analytics Inc., Centrifuge Systems, Future Point Systems, NodeXL and others focus on the insights that can be derived from link analysis, which is easily visualized using relationship graphs – a powerful visual metaphor for showing connections between entities.

Figure 22 VISUAL LANDSCAPE SHIFTS

VISUALIZATION	VISUAL ANALYTICS
Data is displayed	Data is manipulated
Answers	Relationships
Static	Dynamic
User relatively passive	User active
Filter (slice and dice)	Refine and re-analyze
See it	Work it
Data mining	Model mining
Get a result	Make a decision
Single view	Multiple coordinated views
Pie charts, bar charts	Relationship graphs, treemaps, heat maps, bubble charts, timelines
Know what question to ask up front	Questions reveal themselves during analysis

Source: CSC

Relationship graphs were popularized by social networks (see Figure 23) and are increasingly being applied in business. Link analysis and relationships graphs reinforce what Richard May, director of the U.S. National

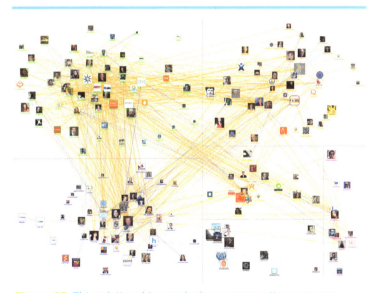

Figure 23 This relationship graph shows connections among Twitter users who mentioned "info360" on March 22, 2011, scaled by number of followers. There are three strong clusters and a more loosely connected fourth cluster in the lower right. (This graph was created using the open source NodeXL social network analysis tool.)

Source: Marc Smith. Licensed under Creative Commons

Visualization and Analytics Center (NVAC), asserts: "We're trying to solve complex problems with complex data in a complex world. While data is the starting place, it's really about analysis and then using visually interactive techniques to identify and follow themes of interest."

Employing an interactive experience, Visual Analytics and Centrifuge enable you to "follow your nose" as entity relationships can be drilled into to reveal more complexities and underlying relationships, which can be seen over time or across space using more traditional visual tools such as time-series graphs and 2D or 3D maps.

The simple example in Figure 24 shows how relationship graphs reveal relationships, making patterns easier to recognize, quantify and act upon. Such visual analysis, combined with comprehensively integrated data sources, including referential sources that supplement analytical sources, can be used to identify high-interest targets. For example, an agency might look at call record data as the analytical source and incorporate referential sources such as subscriber data, case data or other data that adds value to the call records. Due to the extensive associations among all the entities

involved, targets are much more difficult to identify through manual reviews. By using a visual analytics tool such as Visual Analytics' VisuaLinks, much of the manual review is performed automatically.

Centrifuge also provides advanced link analysis and has applied its technology to, among other areas, sales and marketing. Centrifuge has created an application for sales and marketing data to identify performance trends of sales people and marketing tactics. Sources of leads (e.g., digital ads, search engines, email) can be linked to opportunities and sales people to measure sales and marketing effectiveness and guide sales and marketing strategy. (See Figure 25.)

Future Point Systems' Starlight Visual Information System (VIS) software enables people to ingest many forms of data, examine data using 10 different visualizations (see Figure 26), and report their analyses to others in a variety of formats. Analysts can rapidly go from mountains of data to a single clear picture that best tells the story. The core Starlight software originated at the Pacific Northwest National Laboratory, home to NVAC; Future Point Systems in partnership with PNNL has commercialized it.

FRAUD ANALYSIS

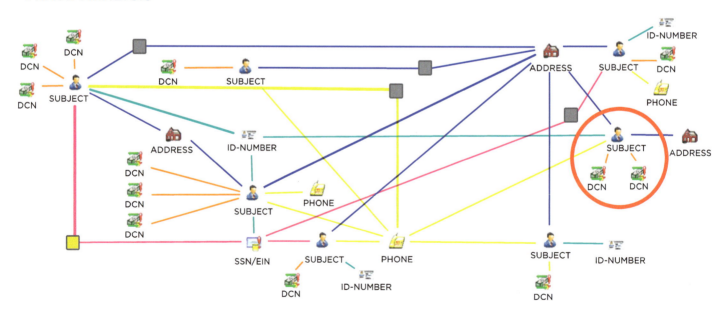

Figure 24 This relationship graph started with two financial reports (denoted DCN) and an associated subject (circled). The network grew as the analyst integrated reports from other states and searched for relationships. Ultimately, the initial subject was found to be involved in an alien smuggling ring; the money was laundered through a used appliance business.
Source: Visual Analytics Inc.

SALES AND MARKETING ALIGNMENT

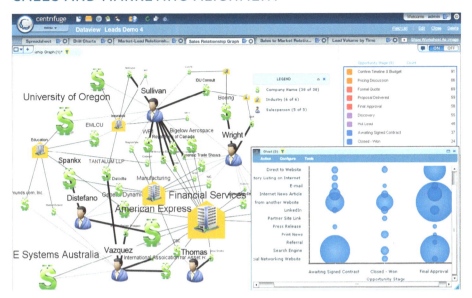

Figure 25 Aligning sales and marketing is essential for success. The graph on the left shows sales people linked to opportunities, including industry. The thicker the line, the higher the probability of closing the deal. The larger the dollar sign, the bigger the deal. Sullivan, Vazquez and Distefano are performing the best. The upper right shows the number of deals by stage in the sales cycle. The blue bubble chart shows potential revenue by marketing program and stage in the sales cycle. Search engine optimization and inbound links from Web sites have the biggest impact.

Armed with this information, marketing managers can advertise to the financial services and manufacturing sectors through specific tactics, and sales managers can see the performance of the reps and the industries where they are successful.

Source: Centrifuge Systems

Figure 26 DATA TAKES ON MANY VIEWS TO PROVIDE NEW LEVELS OF UNDERSTANDING

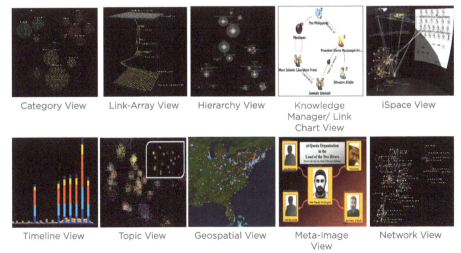

Category View   Link-Array View   Hierarchy View   Knowledge Manager/ Link Chart View   iSpace View

Timeline View   Topic View   Geospatial View   Meta-Image View   Network View

Source: Future Point Systems

These tools, along with those from industry mainstays Spotfire, Tableau, i2 and Hive Group, fall into a new class of analysis that is neither descriptive nor predictive. They are tools that allow people to explore and discover, to examine a hunch, to amplify one's ability to see the data and apply the power of one's visual brain. That hunch, driven by the mind's eye, may lead to the use of rigorous descriptive statistical analysis or the creation of a complex predictive model designed to test the validity of a hypothesis.

MANY DISCIPLINES, MANY MINDS

With the rapid growth in information, "some of the more difficult problems are still ahead of us," says May of NVAC. "Take scale, for example. As you start to scale up, everything starts to break – your ability to interact with the data may not scale, your methodologies to deal with the data may not scale, and even human cognition may not scale. We are quickly entering an era of extreme-scale visual analytics."

To tackle these difficult problems, visual analytics is turning into an interdisciplinary science, going beyond traditional scientific and information visualization to include statistics, mathematics, knowledge representation, management and discovery technologies, cognitive and perceptual sciences, decision sciences, and more. There are many points of view to consider and bring to bear.

The events of 9/11 again bore this out. Following 9/11, the U.S. Department of Homeland Security (DHS) Science and Technology Directorate funded significant efforts that focused on helping analysts make sense of information quickly and efficiently by presenting it visually. NVAC was established to lead the effort and build a community across the public and private sectors to address this.[153]

A framework developed by DHS illustrates how numerous disciplines and techniques are necessary to explore data and achieve a predictive outcome. (See Figure 27.) As Joseph Kielman, the framework's author and Basic/Futures Research Lead for DHS, states, **"Connecting the dots is just one step in, and certainly not sufficient for, understanding any given situation. What is needed is a blending of many methods and minds to tackle the data complexities we are faced with today."**

Many important projects have stemmed from NVAC's efforts. One example is from the GeoVISTA Center, Pennsylvania State University, which has created a visualization platform to help epidemiologists explore the connections between disease, geography and conceptual knowledge. As Figure 28 shows, many important elements such as semantic representation, relationships between concepts, geography, demographics and disease cases are necessary to help gain a rich enough understanding to be able to recognize and manage outbreaks of vector-borne diseases such as malaria and West Nile Virus.

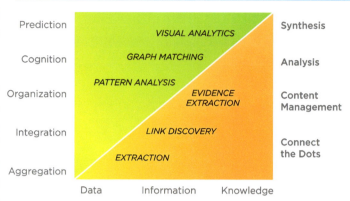

Figure 27 Multiple disciplines and techniques contribute to threat assessment. The same disciplines and techniques apply to all industries when looking for hidden patterns and insights in data.

Source: Joseph Kielman, U.S. Department of Homeland Security

There are also many points of view to consider and bring to bear on these complex problems, leading us to the future of collaborative visual analytics. As researchers have pointed out, "...visual analysis is rarely a solitary activity. Analysts must share and communicate their findings."[154]

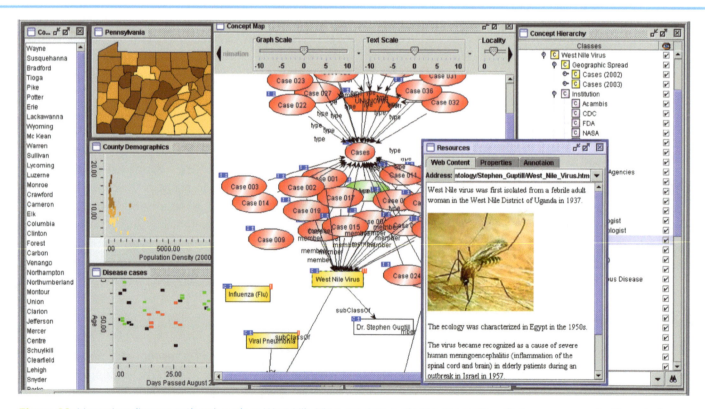

Figure 28 Managing disease outbreak such as West Nile Virus requires exploring connections between conceptual knowledge, geography and disease cases. These disciplines come together using highly coordinated visual representations.

Source: GeoVISTA Center, Pennsylvania State University

There is no better example of this than in law enforcement, where information can come from the intelligence community, law enforcement authorities, other government agencies like transportation and health departments, the private sector and the general public.[155] Bringing visibility to this level of domain sharing is what Visual Analytics has been actively pursuing. For example, Visual Analytics' Data Clarity suite, which incorporates VisuaLinks, provides features and functions to acquire, analyze and share information and intelligence across all levels and sectors of government and private industry. People can simultaneously search all data sources, structured or unstructured (i.e., databases, documents, Web pages), to extract and visually analyze data in numerous ways. This includes clustering, link analysis, timeline analysis, social network analysis, geospatial analysis, entity extraction, classification, ad hoc reporting and data sharing across many disparate organizations at once. (See Figure 29.)

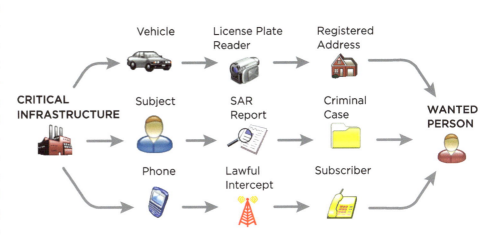

Figure 29 Many different data sources and organizations must collaborate to solve complex problems like criminal investigations. Visualization technologies foster data integration and organizational collaboration, essential for tackling such grand-scale problems.
Source: Visual Analytics Inc.

"Data integration is a critical step towards organization collaboration, with visualization bringing the essential ingredient for insight and awareness around relationships between organizations, data and processes," says Chris Westphal, CEO of Visual Analytics.

Seeing the growth in visualization and the potential for business opportunities, companies like IBM and GE are sponsoring sites that encourage outside participation in creative visualization experiments and contests. IBM's "Many Eyes" Web site is an experiment. It allows anyone to load and share a dataset and then explore the data with a set of visualization tools provided by IBM Cognos.

GE's information challenge site, Visualizing.org, addresses making sense of complex issues through data and design. The focus areas are health, energy and the environment. As the site states, "By giving visual form to the often abstract systemic underpinnings that lie between broad concerns like health, energy, and the environment, we hope to generate actionable knowledge that can be used to improve lives."[156] Importantly, participants are not just technologists but journalists and others digging into public data.

The result has been an explosion of "beautiful data" images and interactive visual designs. It is not just the computer and engineering minds that are engaged but also creative minds from schools of art and design. Today new data-driven techniques are being taught in prestigious art institutions, tooling the next generation of graphic artists with fresh ideas about the use of interactive communication media. Data visualization brings together many disciplines and elements, colorfully captured in Figure 30. The new challenge of data visualization is coming of age and showing signs of progress.

Exploring What's Next. Each year information visualization researchers and practitioners converge at VisWeek to explore new visualization tools, techniques, technologies and theories. VisWeek features the VAST challenge and Vis Contest, which seek novel solutions to real-world data visualization problems. The IEEE VAST 2010 Challenge invited participants to compete in mock data visualization scenarios that included:

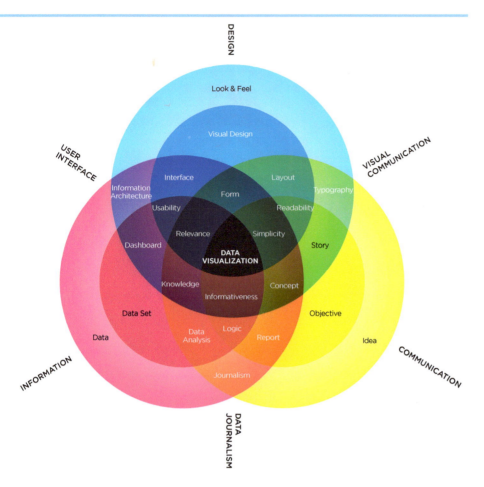

Figure 30 Data visualization brings many disciplines and elements together.

Source: FFunction

- Mini Challenge 1: Text Records – Investigations into Arms Dealing

- Mini Challenge 2: Hospitalization Records – Characterization of Pandemic Spread

- Mini Challenge 3: Genetic Sequences – Tracing the Mutations of a Disease

- Grand Challenge: Combine all data sets – Investigating possible linkage(s) between the illegal arms dealing and the pandemic outbreak

To make it real for the contestants, mock data sets are provided and the solutions are evaluated by leaders in the field.[157]

This year two new symposia will be added to VisWeek focusing on 1) large-scale data analysis and visualization and 2) biological data visualization, reflecting the importance and difficulties posed in these areas.

Overall, there is a new level of exploration and experimentation in the marketplace. Analytics are being applied to any number of public and private data sources, coupled with the orchestration of visual widgetry to give a rich interactive discovery experience – a new phenomenon that is causing an explosion of creativity for visualizing the invisible.

A NEW SENSE OF THINGS TO COME – IMMERSIVE ANALYTICS

The human senses are designed to absorb and analyze data in a 3D world. Our eyes can measure depth of field, our hearing can determine where sounds emanate from, and our touch allows us to control and manipulate objects around us. Yet, the primary interface to computers and electronic data is a 2D screen and rudimentary input devices such as keyboards, touch screens and mice. Can we harness the natural power of our senses to add the human touch required for complex data analysis and reasoning? Yes, by immersing ourselves in the virtual data world, much like we are immersed in the real world – by having the data with us as part of the world we see, by being surrounded by the data and doing discovery, by being inside and looking out.

Analytics are being applied to any number of public and private data sources, coupled with the orchestration of visual widgetry to give a rich interactive discovery experience – a new phenomenon that is causing an explosion of creativity for visualizing the invisible.

New Reality: Augmented Reality.

Recent advances in hardware development have resulted in low-cost miniature sensors, powerful processors, high-capacity batteries and high-resolution visual displays. Together with 3G and 4G wireless technology, a large number of mobile devices – notably smartphones – has emerged that can "augment reality," overlaying visualizations onto the real world. Augmented reality (AR) systems can determine what the most pertinent data is to us in real time based on our location, movements and live camera feeds, ranging from identifying possible military threats for soldiers, to presenting prices of nearby houses for home buyers, to providing information about a tourist area or other site.[158]

Figure 31 This Virtual Tour Guide application, which uses the Argon augmented reality browser, shows the viewer a finished building on his phone when he views a building under construction. The viewer also sees a tweet from a friend and is about to respond. (The inset is an enlarged view of the phone's display.)

Source: Georgia Institute of Technology

Mobile devices will accelerate the adoption of AR. The iPhone was perhaps the first device to raise the specter of AR in the public eye, with its advanced hardware and software libraries available to application developers. However, due to the small screen, it can be difficult to see and quite fiddly to use many current AR applications. New tablet devices with larger screens, such as Apple's iPad 2 and Samsung's Galaxy Tab 10.1 with its open operating system (Android), could be a catalyst for broader adoption of AR technology in the enterprise in the short term.

Another catalyst for broader adoption comes from new AR frameworks that abstract away common components of AR applications from content providers, enabling them to focus on their core business – generating content. KHARMA (KML/HTML Augmented Reality Mobile Architecture), an open source AR framework being developed at the Georgia Institute of Technology, provides common infrastructure required for AR applications such as a user interface (an open source browser called Argon available on the iPhone at the time of writing), "channel servers" that deliver AR content to mobile devices, and services to assist with accurate positioning and identification of buildings and infrastructure.[159] (See Figure 31.) People can focus on creating AR content via familiar tools like HTML, JavaScript and KML (used in Google Earth). Another example is Hoppala, a German company that has released an AR content creation and publishing kit for three major mobile AR browsers: Layar, Junaio and Wikitude.[160]

For people in the field who are mobile and require full use of their hands and limbs, more wearable devices are needed. For example, external devices such as smartphones or tablets would be impractical for soldiers on the ground or maintenance engineers in factories. There is ongoing research to develop AR-capable glasses that people can wear with "head-up" displays overlaying information on the live view. Tanagram is using this technology in the military, while Vuzix is teaming up with Nippon Steel to trial AR glasses in steel plants.[161] Skiers and snowboarders are even being targeted with GPS-enabled goggles that can show speed, distance and location information to the wearer.[162]

Another take on AR is geo-immersion maps, which combine real-time data with digital maps to show, for example, moving traffic and the fastest driving route, or current energy consumption of buildings; researchers at the University of Southern California are exploring geo-immersion and its combination of real and virtual worlds.[163]

Going "Inside the Data" with Immersive Reality. As AR becomes increasingly commercialized, immersive technologies are also making their mark, though chiefly in university settings or highly specialized environments. Most people remember early virtual reality as primitive 3D graphics displayed on large and cumbersome goggles or low-resolution projectors. Immersive Virtual Reality (IVR) technology has evolved significantly since then. Improved processing power and graphic algorithms have reduced lag between people's movements and updates to the visual display. There has also been much work on human interactions, with the virtual world using both active haptics, where motor-driven devices like harnesses provide force feedback in response to a person's movements, as well as passive haptics, where the virtual world is mapped to real life objects.[164] As people move around in the virtual world, they are in fact moving around in the real world; if a person picks up a mug in the real environment, it will get picked up by his avatar in the virtual environment.

Cave Automatic Virtual Environments (or CAVE) have also been created that use high-resolution projectors or large screens set up to surround people. Lightweight 3D glasses replace goggles in these systems; auto-stereo displays, which support glasses-free 3D, are on the way.[165]

IVR has been used extensively in training simulators, where realism and real-time control are important, such as with training military personnel, pilots and rescue crews. The University of New South Wales has set up a CAVE-like environment for mine safety training at the Newcastle Mines Rescue Station. It is used to expose trainees to realistic scenarios without the real-world risk.[166]

The large volumes of data captured in the real world are being used to make virtual environments more realistic. Formula 1 team Marussia Virgin Racing, whose IT and data management infrastructure is supported by CSC, collects approximately 50 gigabytes of data from sensors on the car every race. This data is fed into design and simulation models, including IVR driver simulation environments back at the factory. The simulator is so realistic that the lap times recorded by drivers are within a fraction of a second of actual times during races.

More recently, IVR technology has been applied to data analytics in scientific and biomedical fields. The University of North Carolina at Chapel Hill has set up experiments allowing doctors to perform image-guided biopsies; nanotechnologists

to "feel" nanoparticles as they sense them through atomic force microscopes; and scientists to collaborate on protein crystallography research within the same physical and virtual environment (see Figure 32). With improving network capacity and speeds, it is now possible for multiple groups

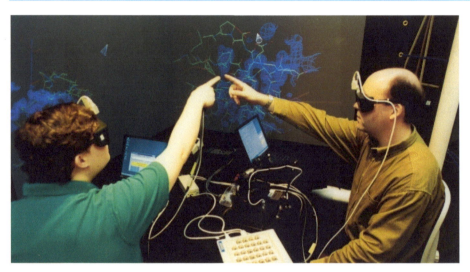

Figure 32 In this immersive virtual reality setting, scientists are collaborating on protein crystallography research.

Source: University of North Carolina at Chapel Hill

to collaborate within CAVEs remotely via their own physical setup.[167] IVR is giving data researchers a massive 3D workbench that everyone can see and use.

This 3D workbench is also exemplified by the AlloSphere, a large, three-story metal sphere inside an echo-free chamber that is being created by a cross-discipline team of researchers at the University of California, Santa Barbara. Up to 20-30 researchers can stand inside the AlloSphere and both see and "hear" their data around them, thus making use of more of their senses than was previously possible. This allows large-scale collaboration not only in terms of the number of researchers in close proximity to each other, but also across disciplines.

The AlloSphere world is created by a collaborative effort from media artists, musicians, engineers and scientists under the direction of professor JoAnn Kuchera-Morin. A number of experiments have been conducted. In one, illustrated in Figure 33, materials professor Chris Van de Walle is working on interactive visualizations

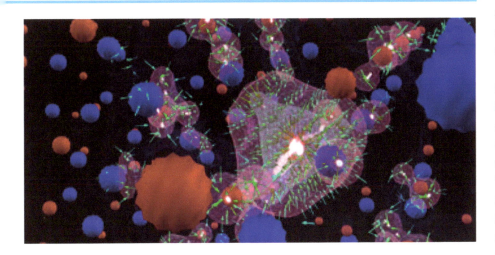

and multimodal representations of unique atomic bonds for alternative energy applications.[168]

Can this technology be applied beyond scientific research? The AlloSphere team believes its tool could be used for a variety of applications, including bioinformatics and "inside-out" geospatial data analysis. Researchers at Duke University have created Redgraph, a virtual reality representation of network data in RDF format (the foundation of linked data), in which people can manipulate graphs in 3D with their hands. Imagine visualizing complex social networks, like the one shown in Figure 23, in three dimensions and picking out trends and patterns.

GAMES LEAD THE WAY FOR INTERACTING WITH THE VIRTUAL WORLD

An ongoing challenge with immersive virtual reality is providing practical and cost-effective human interaction with the virtual environment. With no interactivity, we remain passive participants. Yet to achieve full interactivity often requires expensive, tactile, force-feedback devices and harnesses. While there have been positive results from experiments using less-expensive passive haptics, there is a limit to how big a real-world room can be.

Lessons can be learned from the world of gaming, where effective interactivity is crucial to encourage ongoing play and future purchases. For example, U.S. Army operators are reportedly using hand controllers from game consoles to fly Unmanned Aerial Vehicles (UAVs).[169]

Microsoft's Xbox 360 Kinect add-on is promising to be a highly flexible yet inexpensive input device. Even before the official Microsoft development kit was made available, there were already open source libraries that gave developers access to Kinect's complex inputs, such as hand gestures, body movements, limb and finger movements, and speech.[170] Today there are many applications using this tool. One was created at the Institute of Forensic Medicine at the University of Bern, Switzerland, for surgeons to control cameras during surgery because it is impractical to use standard keyboards, joysticks or controllers.[171]

Perhaps the next challenge for IVR is defining a natural model for interacting with abstract and intangible data. What is the equivalent physical movement for manipulating social graphs or numeric data, and what movements are natural in an immersive world of data?

Visualizing today's data is less about viewing flat passive displays and more about participating with and in the data. To analyze large volumes of diverse data, we need tools to present the data to us in a comprehensible, flexible manner. This could be in the form of social graphs, relationship graphs, geospatial views or some other new visualization. We also have commodity products, ranging from large projectors and screens to smartphones and tablets, that can be used to create data worlds around us through virtual environments and augmented reality. With these technologies we now have an opportunity to add the human touch to data analysis, unleashing our human ingenuity to discover and explore important patterns in the data, leveraging our innate social tendencies to interact, and supporting our need to collaborate in cross-discipline teams.

The Data rEvolution demands that organizations make the most from data in seeking new levels of performance. Organizations should not be content with their own data, though it is an excellent place to start. Insights and new discoveries are to be found both in combining existing data in new ways and in leveraging the data of others. This includes harvesting structured and unstructured data. To this end, a new era of experimentation and innovation is upon us that will bring us into the new realm of the predictive enterprise.

Data continues to open up for experimentation and collective analysis. Organizations are encouraged to "fail forward" because the new technology makes it cheaper, quicker and easier to try and re-try thanks to fast, flexible data models. At the same time, the new data is forging broader collaboration through federated data sets. Data is being shared across boundaries and organizations, be it Toyota (quality and product data), CERN (physics data) or NOAA (ocean data), so that more people can explore and understand the data. (See Figure 34.)

Today, your own data is not enough. For example, it's not enough for financial services to live with its own transactional data; it needs social data to help define and quantify the transactional data further. Similarly, the energy world needs data from NOAA and climate science to better understand energy exploration. These new data connections mean the organization doesn't own all the data. Thus, the idea of Data as a Service – and ultimately Analytics as a Service – starts to make sense because the data needs to

Your own data is not enough.

be available to multiple parties, who need to come together and collaborate on the data.

As data and cloud converge, IT departments need to shift their focus from managing computing infrastructure to helping the organization leverage data for innovation. This includes making data available, providing scalable architectures, adopting cloud storage, and presenting case studies of data-driven business success to business and IT staff.[172]

Great discoveries come from having a broad spectrum of knowledge. The Data rEvolution opens up a world of exciting opportunities for establishing new insights, products, services, partnerships and roles. With data a key factor of production, data's growth and leverage will be a basis for business innovation for years to come. Organizations need to prepare for the data-centered economy.

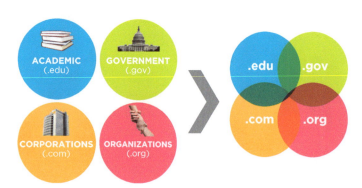

Figure 34 The Data rEvolution brings communities together.
Source: CSC

NOTES

1   "Data, data everywhere," *The Economist*, 25 February 2010, http://www.economist.com/node/15557443?story_id=15557443

2   "Roger Ehrenberg raises big(ger) fund for big data," Fortune.com, 3 December 2010,
    http://finance.fortune.cnn.com/2010/12/03/exclusive-roger-ehrenberg-raises-small-fund-for-big-data/

3   "The Digital Universe Decade – Are You Ready?" IDC, sponsored by EMC Corporation, May 2010. See tab "The Digital Universe Decade,"
    http://www.emc.com/collateral/demos/microsites/idc-digital-universe/iview.htm

4   "EMC's Record Breaking Product Launch," Chuck Hollis blog, 14 January 2011,
    http://chucksblog.emc.com/chucks_blog/2011/01/emcs-record-breaking-product-launch.html

5   Ibid.

6   "Technology Trends You Can't Afford to Ignore," Gartner Webinar, January 2010, slide 8,
    http://www.gartner.com/it/content/1258400/1258425/january_6_techtrends_rpaquet.pdf

7   "James Gleick's History of Information," *The New York Times Sunday Book Review*, 18 March 2011,
    http://www.nytimes.com/2011/03/20/books/review/book-review-the-information-by-james-gleick.html

8   Ibid.

9   "Flash crash update: Why the multi-asset meltdown is a real possibility," *Forbes,* RIABiz blog, 2 March 2011,
    http://blogs.forbes.com/riabiz/2011/03/02/flash-crash-update-why-the-multi-asset-meltdown-is-a-real-possibility/; "Instinet: Boo to the Flash Crash
    Report," *Wall Street Journal MarketBeat blog*, 18 October 2010, http://blogs.wsj.com/marketbeat/2010/10/18/instinet-boo-to-the-flash-crash-report/;
    and "Ex-Physicist Leads Flash Crash Inquiry," *The New York Times*, 20 September 2010,
    http://www.nytimes.com/2010/09/21/business/economy/21flash.html?pagewanted=1&_r=1

10 "Report to the President: Every Federal Agency Needs a 'Big Data' Strategy," *PRNewswire*, 22 March 2011,
    http://m.prnewswire.com/news-releases/report-to-the-president-every-federal-agency-needs-a-big-data-strategy-118433704.html

11 About NCDC's Data, http://www.ncdc.noaa.gov/oa/climate/climateinventories.html#about. See also the NOAA Operational Model Archive and
    Distribution System (NOMADS) project, http://nomads.ncdc.noaa.gov/nomads.php?name=about

12 "Stream Processing of Multi-scale, Near-Real-Time Environmental Data," 15 April 2011, http://www.psc.edu/data-analytics/abstracts/Orcutt.php

13 "Portugal Gives Itself a Clean-Energy Makeover," *The New York Times*, 9 August 2010, http://www.nytimes.com/2010/08/10/science/earth/10portugal.html

14 "The Transition to Intelligent, Secure, Low Carbon, and Climate-Adaptive Infrastructure," compiled by Larry Smarr and Gregory McRae, Australian
    American Leadership Dialogue, 16 July 2010, p. 3, http://lsmarr.calit2.net/repository/Intelligent_Green_Adaptive_Infrastructure_final.pdf

15 Worldwide LHC Computing Grid, http://public.web.cern.ch/public/en/lhc/Computing-en.html

16 Worldwide LHC Computing Grid, Welcome, http://lcg.web.cern.ch/LCG/public/; and What is the Worldwide LHC Computing Grid?
    http://lcg.web.cern.ch/LCG/public/overview.htm

17 Ibid.

18 Worldwide LHC Computing Grid, Grid Computing, http://lcg.web.cern.ch/LCG/public/grid.htm

19 "The Promise and Peril of Big Data," The Aspen Institute, 2010, p. 26, http://www.aspeninstitute.org/publications/promise-peril-big-data

NOTES

20   "EHR-Certification, Semantic Interoperability and the Link to Clinical Research," Prof. Dr. Georges De Moor, President, EuroRec, University of Gent, Belgium, 17 March 2010, http://www.eurorec.org/whoarewe/PR_materials.cfm

21   "Mining Clinical Data: Road to Discovery," *CMIO*, 1 June 2010, http://www.cmio.net/index.php?option=com_articles&view=article&id=22453:mining-clinical-data-road-to-discovery

22   "Credit-Card Rates Climb," *The Wall Street Journal*, 23 August 2010, http://online.wsj.com/article/SB10001424052748704094704575443402132987676.html?mod=ITP_pageone_0

23   "Letting the Machines Decide," *The Wall Street Journal*, 13 July 2010, http://online.wsj.com/article/SB10001424052748703834604575365310813948080.html?KEYWORDS=letting+machines+decide

24   Ibid.

25   Ibid.

26   "CFCT Eyes Rules for Low Latency Colo," *Data Center Knowledge*," 11 June 2010, http://www.datacenterknowledge.com/archives/2010/06/11/cftc-eyes-rules-for-low-latency-colo/

27   Trident Marketing case study from "Operational Analytics: Putting Analytics to Work in Operational Systems," BeyeNETWORK Research Report prepared for Fuzzy Logix, May 2010, pp. 49-52, http://www.beyeresearch.com/study/13489, and communications with Fuzzy Logix.

28   "InsightExpress Rolls Out Data Analytics Cloud from Dell and Aster Data," case study, November 2010, http://www.asterdata.com/resources/assets/cs_InsightExpress_Aster_Data_Dell.pdf

29   "The LinkedIn IPO Millionaires Club," *The Wall Street Journal*, Deal Journal blog, 18 May 2011, http://blogs.wsj.com/deals/2011/05/18/the-linkedin-ipo-millionaires-club/

30   LinkedIn Demographics & Statistics, July 2011, http://www.slideshare.net/amover/linked-in-demographics-statistics-july-2011

31   "Building a terabyte-scale data cycle at LinkedIn with Hadoop and Project Voldemort," LinkedIn SNA Projects Blog, 15 June 2009, http://project-voldemort.com/blog/2009/06/building-a-1-tb-data-cycle-at-linkedin-with-hadoop-and-project-voldemort/

32   "Twitter Seeks $7 Billion Valuation," *The Wall Street Journal*, 6 July 2011, http://online.wsj.com/article/SB10001424052702304803104576428020830361278.html

33   "After Building an Audience, Twitter Turns to Ads," *The New York Times*, 10 October 2010, http://www.nytimes.com/2010/10/11/business/media/11twitter.html; and "Twitter Reaches 155 Million Tweets Per Day," The Realtime Report, 11 April 2011, "http://therealtimereport.com/2011/04/11/twitter-reaches-155-million-tweets-per-day/

34   "The 10+ Best Free Twitter Analytics Tools," The HOB Blog, http://www.thehob.biz/blog/marketing-2/the-10-best-free-twitter-analytics-tools/

35   Michael Stonebraker, "The Case for Shared Nothing," University of California Berkeley, 1985, http://db.cs.berkeley.edu/papers/hpts85-nothing.pdf

36   List of distributed computing projects, http://en.wikipedia.org/wiki/List_of_distributed_computing_projects

37   "Apache Hadoop Wins Terabyte Sort Benchmark," Yahoo! Hadoop Blog, 2 July 2008, http://developer.yahoo.net/blogs/hadoop/2008/07/apache_hadoop_wins_terabyte_sort_benchmark.html

38   Jeffrey Dean and Sanjay Ghemawat, "MapReduce: Simplified Data Processing on Large Clusters," Google Inc., December 2004, http://labs.google.com/papers/mapreduce.html

NOTES

39 "How does Web search (e.g. Google) work?" Armando Fox blog,
  http://www.armandofox.com/geek/computer-questions-asked-by-non-computer-people/how-does-web-search-eg-google-work/

40 Dean and Ghemawat, "MapReduce: Simplified Data Processing on Large Clusters," http://labs.google.com/papers/mapreduce.html

41 Apache Hadoop, http://hadoop.apache.org/

42 Yahoo! Hadoop Blog, http://developer.yahoo.net/blogs/hadoop/

43 "eHarmony Switches from Cloud to Atom Servers," Data Center Knowledge, 10 June 2011,
  http://www.datacenterknowledge.com/archives/2011/06/10/eharmony-switches-from-cloud-to-atom-servers/

44 "Large-Scale Map-Reduce Data Processing at Quantcast," InfoQ, 21 December 2010, http://www.infoq.com/presentations/Map-Reduce-Quantcast

45 "How Rackspace Query Terabytes of Log Data," 30 April 2009,
  http://www.slideshare.net/schubertzhang/case-study-how-rackspace-query-terabytes-of-data-2400928

46 "Hadoop World: Protein Alignment," Paul Brown, 19 November 2009,
  http://www.cloudera.com/blog/2009/11/hadoop-world-protein-alignment-from-paul-brown/

47 "Hadoop World 2010: Hadoop at eBay," 12 October 2010, slide 7, http://www.cloudera.com/resource/hw10_hadoop_at_ebay

48 IBM InfoSphere BigInsights, http://www-01.ibm.com/software/data/infosphere/biginsights/; Greenplum HD Family,
  http://www.greenplum.com/products/greenplum-hd; "Exclusive: Yahoo launching Hadoop spinoff this week," GigaOM, 27 June 2011,
  http://gigaom.com/cloud/exclusive-yahoo-launching-hadoop-spinoff-this-week/; and Hortonworks Manifesto,
  http://www.hortonworks.com/our-manifesto/

49 "MapR Technologies and EMC Announce Technology Licensing Agreement for Next Generation Hadoop Distribution," press release, 25 May 2011,
  http://www.reuters.com/article/2011/05/25/idUS125183+25-May-2011+BW20110525;
  and "MapR to Challenge Cloudera over Hadoop," Sys-Con Media, 30 June 2011, http://www.sys-con.com/node/1891712

50 "Informatica Deal Promises Big Data Impact," InformationWeek, 1 November 2010,
  http://mobile.informationweek.com/10243/show/93f07a604a47d1ee6c3bd2510c8b8790/

51 Hadapt Technology, http://hadapt.squarespace.com/technology/

52 "Big data, but with a familiar face," O'Reilly Radar, 14 December 2010, http://radar.oreilly.com/2010/12/big-data-with-a-familiar-face.html;
  and "Business Analysts Meet Hadoop," ITBusinessEdge, Mike Vizard blog, 14 December 2010,
  http://www.itbusinessedge.com/cm/blogs/vizard/business-analysts-meet-hadoop/?cs=44710

53 "Teradata and Karmasphere Partner to Provide a High-Speed On-Ramp to Big Data," PRNewswire, 26 October 2010,
  http://www.prnewswire.com/news-releases/teradata-and-karmasphere-partner-to-provide-a-high-speed-on-ramp-to-big-data-105762258.html

54 "Update: Teradata to buy marketing vendor Aprimo for $525M," Computerworld, 22 December 2010,
  http://www.computerworld.com/s/article/9202019/Update_Teradata_to_buy_marketing_vendor_Aprimo_for_525M;
  and "Teradata Completes Acquisition of Aster Data," press release, 6 April 2011, http://www.asterdata.com/news/110406-Aster-Data-Teradata.php

55 "Pioneers in Ad hoc Reporting Platform to support Hadoop framework for Large Data analysis via Hive and Aster Data," press release, 3 June 2010,
  http://www.intellicus.com/about/news_room/news_room.htm?_kk=large%20data%20reporting&_kt=d2ca56f8-f5d8-459f-9a2e-3c211550c7e5&gclid=
  CIaU162Oq6cCFUUb6wodEiXQAw

56 Splunk FISMA Compliance, http://www.splunk.com/view/fisma-compliance/SP-CAAACPP, and communications with Splunk.

NOTES

57   Apache Pig, http://hadoop.apache.org/pig/; and Cascading, http://www.cascading.org/

58   "EMC, NetApp Make It a Big Day for Big Data Star Hadoop," GigaOM, 9 May 2011,
      http://gigaom.com/cloud/emc-netapp-make-it-a-big-day-for-big-data-star-hadoop/; and "NetApp Unveils New Portfolio of Products and Solutions to
      Tackle Big-Bandwidth and High-Performance Applications," press release, 9 May 2011,
      http://www.netapp.com/us/company/news/news-rel-20110509-692530.html

59   S4: Distributed Stream Computing Platform, http://s4.io/; and Leonardo Neumeyer, Bruce Robbins, Anish Nair and Anand Kesari, "S4: Distributed
      Stream Computing Platform," Yahoo! Labs, 2010, http://labs.yahoo.com/files/KDCloud%202010%20S4.pdf

60   NoSQL Databases, http://nosql-database.org/

61   Apache Hadoop, http://hadoop.apache.org/

62   Yahoo! Developer Network, http://developer.yahoo.com/hadoop/

63   Giuseppe DeCandia et al., "Dynamo: Amazon's Highly Available Key-value Store," Amazon.com, 2007,
      http://s3.amazonaws.com/AllThingsDistributed/sosp/amazon-dynamo-sosp2007.pdf

64   Fay Chang et al., "Bigtable: A Distributed Storage System for Structured Data," Google Inc., 2006,
      http://static.googleusercontent.com/external_content/untrusted_dlcp/labs.google.com/en/us/papers/bigtable-osdi06.pdf;
      and "Apache Hadoop Wins Terabyte Sort Benchmark," Yahoo! Hadoop Blog, 2 July 2008,
      http://developer.yahoo.net/blogs/hadoop/2008/07/apache_hadoop_wins_terabyte_sort_benchmark.html

65   Facebook Developers – Graph API, http://developers.facebook.com/docs/reference/api/ (Requires sign-in.)

66   Foursquare & MongoDB, 21 May 2010, https://docs.google.com/present/view?id=dhkkqm6q_13gm6jq5fv

67   "Deriving deep customer insights using MongoDB," http://www.10gen.com/video/mongosv2010/intuit

68   Who is Using Riak, http://wiki.basho.com/Who-is-Using-Riak.html

69   "Holy Large Hadron Collider, Batman!" MongoDB NoSQL Database Blog, 3 June 2010, http://blog.mongodb.org/post/660037122/holy-large-hadron-collider-batman;
      and "CERN – CouchDB and Physics," http://www.couchbase.com/case-studies/cern

70   The ACID Model, http://databases.about.com/od/specificproducts/a/acid.htm. See also Theo Haerder and Andreas Reuter, "Principles of Transaction-
      Oriented Database Recovery," ACM Computing Surveys 15 (4), December 1983, pp. 287–317,
      http://portal.acm.org/ft_gateway.cfm?id=291&type=pdf&coll=GUIDE&dl=GUIDE&CFID=18545439&CFTOKEN=99113095.
      "These four properties, atomicity, consistency, isolation, and durability (ACID), describe the major highlights of the transaction paradigm, which has
      influenced many aspects of development in database systems."

71   Gartner, Market Share: All Software Markets, Worldwide, 2010, 30 March 2011, ID:G00211976.

72   Despite the title of this article, it reaffirms the staying power of relational databases – and this was four years ago. "Pioneer calls RDBMS technology
      obsolete," Techworld, 7 September 2007, http://news.techworld.com/applications/10018/pioneer-calls-rdbms-technology-obsolete/

73   Database.com, http://www.database.com/what, and Database.com blog, http://blog.database.com/.
      Also see DaaS on list of predictions for 2011, http://m.zdnet.com/blog/service-oriented/big-data-for-the-year-ahead-10-predictions/6258

74   Database.com FAQ, http://wiki.database.com/page/FAQ

NOTES

75 "Big Opportunities for Startups Providing Big Data, Data-as-a-Service," ReadWriteWeb, 9 December 2010,
http://www.readwriteweb.com/start/2010/12/big-opportunities-for-startups.php

76 Communications with EMC Greenplum.

77 "Aster Data Customer Examples," slide 7, and communications with Aster Data.

78 Oracle Exadata Database Machine X2-8 data sheet,
http://www.oracle.com/technetwork/database/exadata/dbmachine-x2-8-datasheet-173705.pdf?ssSourceSiteId=ocomen

79 "AOL installs 50TB of SSD; boosts DB performance by 4X," Computerworld, 14 October 2010,
http://www.computerworld.com/s/article/9191079/AOL_installs_50TB_of_SSD_boosts_DB_performance_by_4X

80 Acunu Data Platform, http://www.acunu.com/products/

81 "Acunu Reinvents the Data Stack for Big Data," BusinessWire, 23 June 2011,
http://www.businesswire.com/news/home/20110623005234/en/Acunu-Reinvents-Data-Stack-Big-Data; and "Exclusive: Big Data Startup Acunu Raises
Small Funding," GigaOM, 23 February 2011, http://gigaom.com/cloud/exclusive-big-data-startup-acunu-raises-small-funding/

82 Real-Time Analytics with SAP HANA Computing, http://www36.sap.com/platform/in-memory-computing/in-memory-appliance/index.epx;
SAP HANA system architecture, February 2011, http://www.scribd.com/doc/53821654/; and "FAQ: SAP's HANA in-memory computing platform,"
Computerworld, 20 May 2011, http://www.computerworld.com/s/article/9216903/FAQ_SAP_s_HANA_in_memory_computing_platform

83 VMware GemFire presentation (partner training)

84 VoltDB Products, http://voltdb.com/content/how-voltdb-works

85 Alpine Miner data sheet, http://www.alpinedatalabs.com/assets/files/AlpineMinerDatasheet.pdf

86 "EMC lets go of Greenplum Community Edition," The Register, 1 February 2011,
http://www.theregister.co.uk/2011/02/01/emc_greenplum_community_edition/, http://madlib.net/

87 "NoSQL: Is It Time to Ditch Your Relational Database?" Andrew Whitehouse's Weblog, 24 April 2010,
http://andrewwhitehouse.wordpress.com/2010/04/24/nosql-is-it-time-to-ditch-your-relational-database/

88 "Membase-Cloudera Integration Joins Leading Hadoop Distribution and Real-Time NoSQL Database," press release, 12 October 2010,
http://www.cloudera.com/company/press-center/releases/membase-cloudera_integration_joins_leading_hadoop_distribution_and_real-time_nosql_database

89 Brisk, http://www.datastax.com/products/brisk

90 "I'll Take Hadoop for $400, Alex," Yahoo! Hadoop Blog, 24 February 2011,
http://developer.yahoo.com/blogs/hadoop/posts/2011/02/i%E2%80%99ll-take-hadoop-for-400-alex/

91 "EMC to Acquire Greenplum," press release, 6 July 2010, http://www.emc.com/about/news/press/2010/20100706-01.htm

92 "Hadoop Gets Commercial Cred as Cloudera and Netezza Connect," GigaOM, 15 July 2010,
http://gigaom.com/2010/07/15/hadoop-gets-commercial-cred-as-cloudera-and-netezza-connect/

93 Netflix Prize, http://www.netflixprize.com/; and BellKor's Pragmatic Chaos, http://www2.research.att.com/~volinsky/netflix/bpc.html

94 "$3 Million Health Care Analytics Challenge," ReadWriteWeb, 16 December 2010,
http://www.readwriteweb.com/hack/2010/12/3-million-prize-for-health-car.php#

NOTES

95   "Amazon patents procedure to let recipients avoid undesirable gifts," *The Seattle Times*, 27 December 2010,
     http://seattletimes.nwsource.com/html/businesstechnology/2013781512_amazon28.html

96   "Info Systems Must 'Connect Dots' on Terrorism," *Defense News*, 19 April 2010,
     http://www.defensenews.com/story.php?i=4588125, http://www.orgnet.com/prevent.html

97   "Analyzing Literature by Words and Numbers," *The New York Times*, 3 December 2010, http://www.nytimes.com/2010/12/04/books/04victorian.html;
     and "Digital Keys for Unlocking the Humanities' Riches," *The New York Times*, 16 November 2010, http://www.nytimes.com/2010/11/17/arts/17digital.html

98   How People Use Recorded Future, https://www.recordedfuture.com/how-to-use-media-analytics.html; and "Recorded Future Knows Tomorrow – Already,"
     Everything PR, 1 November 2010, http://www.pamil-visions.net/recorded-future/220603/

99   Yanlei Diao et al., "Capturing Data Uncertainty in High-Volume Stream Processing," 10 September 2009, http://cdsweb.cern.ch/record/1206014

100 "$150 Billion Money Manager Builds Real-Time Analytics," *Windows in Financial Services*, Summer 2006,
     http://www.streambase.com/pdf/WIFS_RealTimeAnalytics_StreamBase.pdf

101 IBM InfoSphere Streams Use Cases presentation, 12 April 2011,
     https://www-304.ibm.com/partnerworld/wps/servlet/mem/ContentHandler/U898588B23086J52 (Requires sign-in.)

102 "Preview of Storm: The Hadoop of Realtime Processing," BackType Technology,
     http://tech.backtype.com/preview-of-storm-the-hadoop-of-realtime-proce;
     and "A Preview of Storm: an exciting development in streaming Hadoop," QuantLabs.net, 30 May 2011,
     http://quantlabs.net/labs/articles/quant-development/1169-a-preview-of-storm-an-exciting-development-in-streaming-hadoop

103 Tyson Condie et al., "Online Aggregation and Continuous Query support in MapReduce," SIGMOD '10, 6-11 June 2010,
     http://neilconway.org/docs/sigmod2010_hop_demo.pdf; and "Enabling Hadoop Batch Processing Systems to Consume Streaming Data," Yahoo!
     Hadoop Blog, 9 June 2010, http://developer.yahoo.com/blogs/hadoop/posts/2010/06/enabling_hadoop_batch_processi_1/

104 "Trending: Crowdflow.net," W5 blog, 18 May 2011, http://w5blog.com/2011/05/18/trending-crowdflow-net-2/

105 https://simplegeo.com/

106 "Study finds Netflix is the largest source of internet traffic in North America," Engadget, 17 May 2011,
     http://www.engadget.com/2011/05/17/study-finds-netflix-is-the-largest-source-of-internet-traffic-in/

107 "Details of 'Einstein' Cyber Shield Disclosed by White House," *The Wall Street Journal*, Digits blog, 2 March 2010,
     http://blogs.wsj.com/digits/2010/03/02/%E2%80%9Ceinstein%E2%80%9D-program-disclosed-as-us-cyber-shield/

108 http://www.freebase.com/; and "Google acquires MetaWeb; says Freebase will become 'more open,'" VentureBeat, 16 July 2010,
     http://deals.venturebeat.com/2010/07/16/google-acquires-metaweb-says-freebase-will-become-more-open/

109 Google Image Labeler, http://images.google.com/imagelabeler/; ESP Game, http://en.wikipedia.org/wiki/ESP_game;
     and Gwap, http://www.gwap.com/gwap/about/

110 IBM Integrated Information Core, Version 1.4.0, Reference Semantic Model,
     http://publib.boulder.ibm.com/infocenter/iicdoc/v1r4m0/index.jsp (Insert "reference semantic model" in the search box.)

111 "Final Jeopardy: How can Watson conclude that Toronto is a U.S. city?" Stephen Baker's blog, 15 February 2011,
     http://thenumerati.net/?postID=726&final-jeopardy-how-can-watson-conclude-that-toronto-is-a-u-s-city

NOTES

112 Linked Data and Gov 2.0 Expo 2010, see video at [9:45],
http://blogstats.wordpress.com/2011/02/24/linked-data-its-not-a-top-down-system-berners-lee-and-opengov/.
See also "Tim Berners-Lee and Group of Boston Web Gurus Leading New MIT Class to Get Linked Data to Market," Xconomy, 16 June 2010,
http://www.xconomy.com/boston/2010/06/16/tim-berners-lee-and-group-of-boston-web-gurus-leading-new-mit-class-to-get-linked-data-movement-to-the-market/

113 "Clinical Quality Linked Data on Health.data.gov," 9 June 2011, http://www.data.gov/communities/node/81/blogs/4920

114 http://www.epa.gov/narel/radnet/

115 "W3C Cuts Path for Global Government Linked Data (GLD)," CMSWire, 14 June 2011,
http://www.cmswire.com/cms/information-management/w3c-cuts-path-for-global-government-linked-data-gld-011615.php

116 LinkedCT, http://linkedct.org/about/

117 Ibid.

118 Oktie Hassanzadeh, M.Sc., Anastasios Kementsietsidis, Ph.D., Lipyeow Lim, Ph.D., Renée J. Miller, Ph.D., Min Wang, Ph.D., University of Toronto and IBM T.J. Watson Research Center, "LinkedCT: A Linked Data Space for Clinical Trials," 2009, pp. 2-3,
ftp://ftp.cs.toronto.edu/pub/reports/csri/596/LinkedCT.pdf

119 "How to 'Connect the Dots' in Your Business," Tom Davenport, HBR Blog Network, 26 January 2010,
http://blogs.hbr.org/davenport/2010/01/eight_steps_to_connecting_the.html

120 This notion of integrating structured and unstructured data sets is referred to as Unified Information Access. UIA is about combining business intelligence and search techniques to provide more context and get more meaningful results, including connections in the data you didn't know existed (i.e., questions you didn't know to ask). An interesting discussion about this ability to connect the dots, not just find them, is at
http://www.attivio.com/blog/57-unified-information-access/767-finding-dots-vs-connecting-dots.html

121 "Business, IT collaboration drives new BI system at Toyota," Computerworld, 4 May 2011,
http://www.computerworld.com/s/article/9216390/Business_IT_collaboration_drives_new_BI_system_at_Toyota?taxonomyId=9&pageNumber=1, and communications with Endeca.

122 "Gartner Announces Finalists of the 2011 Business Intelligence Excellence Awards," press release, 13 April 2011, http://www.gartner.com/it/page.jsp?id=1631315

123 "Person of the Year 2010: Mark Zuckerberg," Time, 15 December 2010,
http://www.time.com/time/specials/packages/article/0,28804,2036683_2037183_2037185,00.html;
and Facebook Facebooking page, http://www.facebook.com/pages/Facebook-Statistics/146281928724857. Data reported is as of July 2011.

124 "Mining the Web for Feelings, Not Facts," The New York Times, 23 August 2009,
http://www.nytimes.com/2009/08/24/technology/internet/24emotion.html?_r=2&adxnnl=1&adxnnlx=1292000589-eUyWLMpbfxCnnVMLHavB1w

125 "Connecting the Dots: Tracking Two Identified Terrorists," orgnet.com, 2008, http://www.orgnet.com/prevent.html

126 "Pampers takes on mommy bloggers and wins," Social Media Influence, 10 May 2010,
http://socialmediainfluence.com/2010/05/10/pampers-takes-on-mommy-bloggers-and-wins/

127 "Exalead Extends Search-based Application Leadership with Exalead CloudView 360 Introduction," press release, 9 December 2010,
http://www.exalead.com/software/news/press-releases/2010/12-09.php

NOTES

128   "Wall St. Computers Read the News, and Trade on It," *The New York Times*, 21 December 2010,
      http://www.nytimes.com/2010/12/22/technology/22trading.html?_r=1

129   About Appinions, http://appinions.com/about/; and "Get Familiar with the Term 'IRM,'" Appinions blog, 10 August 2011, http://appinions.com/blog/

130   Lithium, Who We Are, http://www.lithium.com/who-we-are/

131   For more on earlier detection, see "The Future of Healthcare: It's Health, Then Care," CSC Leading Edge Forum, December 2010, pp. 16-21,
      http://assets1.csc.com/lef/downloads/LEF_2010FutureofHealthcare.pdf

132   Jeremy Ginsberg, Matthew H. Mohebbi, Rajan S. Patel, Lynnette Brammer, Mark S. Smolinski and Larry Brilliant, "Detecting influenza epidemics using
      search engine query data," Google Inc. and Centers for Disease Control and Prevention, *Nature* 457, 19 February 2009, pp. 1012-1014,
      http://www.nature.com/nature/journal/v457/n7232/full/nature07634.html (Requires sign-in.)
      The article and more about how this works are also here: http://www.google.org/flutrends/about/how.html

133   "It's flu o'clock somewhere," Google.org blog, 8 June 2010, http://blog.google.org/2010/06/its-flu-oclock-somewhere.html

134   Google Flu Trends FAQ, "Will Google Flu Trends someday include other diseases?" http://www.google.org/flutrends/about/faq.html

135   "The Web's Cutting Edge, Anonymity in Name Only," *The Wall Street Journal*, "What They Know" series, 4 August 2010,
      http://online.wsj.com/article/SB10001424052748703294904575385532109190198.html?mod=WSJ_hps_MIDDLEThirdNews

136   iovation Solutions Overview, http://www.iovation.com/solutions/; iovation video: ReputationManager,
      http://www.iovation.com/iov-video/; and "Race Is On to 'Fingerprint' Phones, PCs," *The Wall Street Journal*, "What They Know" series,
      30 November 2010, http://online.wsj.com/article/SB10001424052748704679204575646704100959546.html

137   "GridGlo Mines Big Data for Real Time Energy Apps," GigaOM, 10 May 2011,
      http://gigaom.com/cleantech/gridglo-mines-big-data-for-real-time-energy-apps/

138   Google Instant, http://www.google.com/instant/; and "Google Unveils Tool to Speed Up Searches," *The New York Times*, 8 September 2010,
      http://www.nytimes.com/2010/09/09/technology/techspecial/09google.html?_r=1&scp=1&sq=google%20instant&st=cse

139   Peter Norvig, "Natural Language Corpus," in *Beautiful Data*, ed. Toby Segaran and Jeff Hammerbacher (O'Reilly Media, Inc., 2009), pp. 219-242;
      and "The Renaissance man: how to become a scientist over and over again," *Discover*, 8 June 2011,
      http://mblogs.discovermagazine.com/notrocketscience/2011/06/08/the-renaissance-man-how-to-become-a-scientist-over-and-over-again/

140   Clayton Christensen, *The Innovator's Dilemma: When New Technologies Cause Great Firms to Fail* (Harvard Business School Press: Boston, 1997), p. xv.
      "Products based on disruptive technologies are typically cheaper, simpler, smaller, and, frequently, more convenient to use."

141   Famous Quotes and Quotations, http://www.famous-quotes-and-quotations.com/yogi-berra-quotes.html

142   Dennis P. Culhane et al., "Connecting the Dots: The Promise of Integrated Data Systems for Policy Analysis and Systems Reform," Intelligence for
      Social Policy, Vol 1. No. 3, 22 March 2010, http://works.bepress.com/cgi/viewcontent.cgi?article=1089&context=dennis_culhane

143   "In New Military, Data Overload Can Be Deadly," *The New York Times*, 16 January 2011, http://www.nytimes.com/2011/01/17/technology/17brain.html?_r=1

144   "Charles R. Troyer, "Forecasting in a More Uncertain World," CSC white paper, 2010,
      http://www.csc.com/consumer_goods_and_services/insights/56138-forecasting_in_a_more_uncertain_world

NOTES

145 "Complex, Multi-Dimensional Data Sets Pose Special Challenges for Financial Services Firms," Revolution Analytics case study, 2010, http://www.revolutionanalytics.com/why-revolution-r/case-studies/Bank-of-America-Case-Study.pdf

146 R data sheet, http://www.revolutionanalytics.com/products/pdf/RevoScaleR.pdf; Lee Edlefsen, "RevoScaleR Speed and Scalability," Revolution Analytics white paper, 2011, http://www.revolutionanalytics.com/why-revolution-r/whitepapers/RevoScaleR-Speed-Scalability.pdf; RHIPE – R and Hadoop Integrated Processing Environment," http://www.stat.purdue.edu/~sguha/rhipe/; and "Revolution Analytics Brings Big Data Analysis to R," press release, 3 August 2010, http://www.revolutionanalytics.com/news-events/news-room/2010/revolution-analytics-brings-big-data-analysis-to-R.php

147 "Business intelligence moves to the iPad, iPhone," *Computerworld*, 6 July 2010, http://www.computerworld.com/s/article/9178882/Business_intelligence_moves_to_the_iPad_iPhone; Roambi, http://www.roambi.com/; and "San Diego start-up raises $10 million," *The San Diego Union-Tribune*, 21 December 2010, http://www.signonsandiego.com/news/2010/dec/21/san-diego-start-up-raises-10-million/)

148 "BigSheets: extending business intelligence through web data," http://www-01.ibm.com/software/ebusiness/jstart/bigsheets/

149 Datameer Analytics Solution, http://www.kdnuggets.com/2010/10/datameer-analytics-solution.html; and "Closing the gap between big data and people who need it," O'Reilly Radar, 10 December 2010, http://radar.oreilly.com/2010/12/closing-the-gap-between-big-da.html

150 "Google Integrates BigQuery with Google Apps Script and Google Spreadsheets," ReadWriteWeb, 7 January 2011, http://www.readwriteweb.com/hack/2011/01/google-integrates-bigquery-with-google-apps-script-and-google-spreadsheets.php#

151 "Google BigQuery gets scripting and spreadsheets," I Programmer, 11 January 2011, http://www.i-programmer.info/news/141-cloud-computing/1819-google-bigquery-gets-scripting-and-spreadsheets.html

152 "Massive Health Uses Big Data, Mobile Phones to Fight Chronic Disease," GigaOM, 2 February 2011, http://gigaom.com/2011/02/02/massive-health-uses-big-data-mobile-phones-to-fight-chronic-disease/

153 See the Visual Analytics Community, www.vacommunity.org.

154 Jeffrey Heer and Maneesh Agrawala, University of California, Berkeley, "Design considerations for collaborative visual analytics," Information Visualization (2008) 7, pp. 49-62, http://citeseerx.ist.psu.edu/viewdoc/download?doi=10.1.1.168.4282&rep=rep1&type=pdf

155 National Criminal Intelligence Sharing Plan, U.S. Department of Justice, October 2003, http://it.ojp.gov/ncisp

156 Visualizing.org, http://www.visualizing.org/issues (accessed 26 June 2011)

157 See http://hcil.cs.umd.edu/localphp/hcil/vast10/index.php to download a sample data set.

158 "Precise overlay registration within Augmented Reality – a glimpse into the technology," Tanagram's Spill blog, http://spill.tanagram.com/2010/05/24/precise-overlay-registration-within-augmented-reality-a-glimpse-into-the-technology/; and The CommBank 3D Reader, Commonwealth Bank Group, http://www.commbank.com.au/personal/home-loans/3d-reader.aspx

159 KHARMA Framework, https://research.cc.gatech.edu/kharma/content/kharma-framework; and Argon Browser, http://argonbrowser.org/

160 "Hoppala AR Content Platform opens to all major mobile ar browsers," 7 March 2011, http://www.hoppala-agency.com/category/augmentation

161 "Precise overlay registration within Augmented Reality – a glimpse into the technology," Tanagram's Spill blog, http://spill.tanagram.com/2010/05/24/precise-overlay-registration-within-augmented-reality-a-glimpse-into-the-technology/; and "Vuzix and NS Solutions Corporation Partner to Deliver Augmented Reality Solutions For Manufacturing," press release, 24 February 2011, http://www.vuzix.com/site/_news/Press%20Release%20NS%20SOL%20Partnership%2002-24-2011%20-%20Final.pdf

NOTES

162   Zeal Optics Transcend GPS Goggle, https://www.zealoptics.com/transcend/

163   "USC computer scientist makes geo-immersion maps, leaves other maps feeling inferior," Engadget, 13 July 2011,
      http://www.engadget.com/2011/07/13/usc-computer-scientist-makes-geo-immersion-maps-other-maps-left/

164   "What's Really Real About Immersive Virtual Reality?" Fred Brooks, University of North Carolina at Chapel Hill, TTI/Vanguard presentation, 7 December 2010.

165   CAVE Automatic Virtual Environment, http://en.wikipedia.org/wiki/Cave_Automatic_Virtual_Environment;
      and Immersive Visualization Lab Infrastructure, Calit2, http://ivl.calit2.net/wiki/index.php/Infrastructure

166   Virtual Reality Simulator, UNSW School of Mining Engineering,
      http://www.mining.unsw.edu.au/information-for/future-students/future-undergraduates/what-mining/virtual-reality-simulator

167   "Mixed Virtual/Physical Collaboration Spaces at Calit2: Collapsing the 'Flat' World to a Single Point," Web article, 19 May 2010,
      http://www.calit2.net/newsroom/article.php?id=1686

168   Research in the AlloSphere, http://www.allosphere.ucsb.edu/research.php; and TED 2009 presentation, [3:21],
      http://www.allosphere.ucsb.edu/media.php

169   "Photos: The Army's vision for soldier tech," ZDNet, 28 May 2007,
      http://www.zdnet.com/photos/photos-the-armys-vision-for-soldier-tech/67546?seq=10&tag=photo-frame;get-photo-roto

170   "Using the Kinect gets much easier," I Programmer, 11 December 2010,
      http://www.i-programmer.info/news/91-hardware/1688-using-the-kinect-gets-much-easier.html

171   "Boffins build medical control centre with Kinect," Register Hardware, December 2010, http://www.reghardware.com/2010/12/23/vitopsy_kinect/

172   "The Internet of Things and the Cloud CIO of the Future," CIO, 4 January 2011,
      http://www.cio.com/article/651166/The_Internet_of_Things_and_the_Cloud_CIO_of_the_Future

ACKNOWLEDGMENTS

The Leading Edge Forum gives special recognition to Walt Mullikin, Sidney Shek and Lisa Braun for their significant contributions to *Data rEvolution*. Walt, a leading practitioner in business intelligence, devoted countless hours of study and reflection on the data revolution as it relates to his practice. After working on a CSC grant on NoSQL, Sidney played a key role in ensuring technology and architectural completeness throughout the report. Lisa, as senior writer, synthesized all the perspectives and conveyed them in a powerful style to promote dialogue and learning.

The LEF also thanks the following for their contribution to *Data rEvolution*:

Tony Agresta, *Centrifuge Systems*

Ian Andrews, *Aster Data*

Vince Barrett, *Centrifuge Systems*

Jarrod Bassan, *CSC*

Paul Beduhn, *Vision Chain*

Alex Black, *CSC*

Fred Brooks, *University of North Carolina, Chapel Hill*

David Brown, *VMware*

Sujan Debnath, *CSC*

Mike Elashoff, *CardioDx*

Jeff Erhardt, *Revolution Analytics*

Cyrus Golkar, *Fuzzy Logix*

Rosemary Hartman, *CSC*

Sharon Hays, *CSC*

Jason Hines, *Recorded Future*

Jeanne Holm, *Data.gov*

Ian Jackson, *CSC*

Joseph Kielman, *U.S. Department of Homeland Security*

Les Klein, *CSC*

JoAnn Kuchera-Morin, *University of California, Santa Barbara*

Conrad Lautenbacher, *CSC*

Ed Luczak, *CSC*

Alan MacEachren, *Pennsylvania State University*

Rob Massoudi, *Space-Time Insight*

Richard May, *National Visualization and Analytics Center*

Peter Mayall, *CSC*

Dan Munyan, *CSC*

KeeSiong Ng, *EMC*

David O'Connor, *Visual Analytics Inc.*

Scott Rayder, *CSC*

Rus Records, *CSC*

Rob Schilling, *Space-Time Insight*

Shyamal Sen, *CSC*

Tony Shaw, *Dataversity*

Ben Shneiderman, *University of Maryland*

Tom Soderstrom, *NASA Jet Propulsion Laboratory*

Paul Sonderegger, *Endeca*

Hal Stern, *Juniper Networks*

Albert Tang, *CSC*

Tony Tedesco, *CSC*

Rick Tomredle, *CSC*

Omer Trajman, *Cloudera*

Michael Tran, *CSC*

Charles Troyer, *CSC*

Fran Turisco, *CSC*

Gaurav Tyagi, *CSC*

Mike Upchurch, *Fuzzy Logix*

Daisy Weaver, *CSC*

Chris Westphal, *Visual Analytics Inc.*

Justin Wolf, *Future Point Systems*

Tim Young, *Splunk*